CALIFORNIA DMV

WRITTEN TEST 2024

(400 Questions With Explained Answers)

A Simple And Easy To Follow Guide, Includes

Pictures For Easy Understanding

Precision Driving School

DEDICATION

This book is devoted to every ambitious driver who is on a mission to understand the laws of the road and gain the right to cruise along California's highways and byways.

May your passion to study and safety be your guides on the journey ahead. This book is meticulously constructed to walk you through the many facets of driving, ensuring that you not only pass the California DMV Written Test but also become a responsible and competent driver.

Best wishes and safe travels on your journey to become a confident and proficient driver.

Table of Contents

INTRODUCTION

The California DMV Written Test is an important stage in earning a driver's license since it assesses a person's understanding of road regulations, traffic legislation, and safe driving practices. This test is meant to verify that drivers have the essential abilities and knowledge to drive safely on California roadways. This written exam is designed to assess your comprehension of driving duties and rules, increasing road safety for all motorists and pedestrians.

The purpose of the California DMV written test

Assessing Knowledge: The exam is designed to assess your knowledge of California's traffic laws, road signs, and driving restrictions. This contains an assessment of your understanding of right-of-way laws, speed limits, parking restrictions, and other topics.

boosting Safe Driving Practices: By assessing your understanding of defensive driving concepts and how to manage diverse driving scenarios, the DMV hopes to guarantee that you are prepared to make wise judgments on the road, reducing the likelihood of accidents and boosting overall road safety.

Legal Compliance: Knowing the California Vehicle Code is critical for all drivers. The written exam measures your knowledge with essential areas of the code, ensuring that you understand the legal requirements and penalties of driving offenses.

How This Book Can Help You Pass With Confidence

complete Coverage: This book covers all of the important subjects covered on the California DMV Written Test, serving as a complete resource to help you grasp the content.

Full Explanations: Each question in the practice exams is accompanied by a full explanation, which will help you understand the logic behind the right answer. This guarantees that you not only recall data but also fully appreciate the concepts regulating safe and responsible driving.

Realistic Practice Exams: The included practice exams replicate the structure and difficulty level of the real DMV Written Test, enabling you to get acquainted with the testing environment and evaluate your preparation.

strategy Study Approach: The book is organized to walk you through each important part of the written exam, providing a strategy study approach. By concentrating on individual chapters and practising with example questions, you may gain confidence and skill in all areas.

Understanding the DMV test format.

The California DMV Written Test is designed to test your understanding of traffic regulations, road signs, and safe driving techniques. Familiarization with the exam format is essential for good preparation. The test is often made up of multiple-choice questions covering a broad variety of California driving-related subjects. To assist you succeed, the questions are organized into topics such as traffic regulations, road rules, defensive driving, and more.

Key Features of the DMV Written Test Format:

Multiple-Choice Questions: The bulk of the exam questions are given in multiple-choice style, with various alternatives available for each question. Your objective is to choose the right answer from the options provided.

The exam covers a wide variety of issues, including traffic signals, right-of-way laws, parking restrictions, and unique driving scenarios. This variety guarantees that you have a comprehensive grasp of California's traffic rules.

Number of Questions: The actual number of questions on the exam may vary, but it usually has a defined number of questions. To pass the exam, you must get a certain proportion of right answers.

Passing Score: The passing score varies, and you should be informed of the minimal percentage needed to receive your learner's permit or driver's license.

How This Book Will Help You Pass The Exam 100%

This thorough guide has been deliberately designed to improve your chances of passing the California DMV Written Test. Here's how this book will help you prepare for a perfect score.

In-depth Content Coverage

This book covers all of the subjects required for the written exam, including traffic regulations, defensive driving, and more. Each chapter is designed to improve your grasp of the content, ensuring you are familiar with all aspects of California driving legislation.

Explanation of Answers:

Every practice exam in this book has detailed answers. This means that each question includes not just the right answer but also a detailed explanation of why it is correct. Understanding the logic behind each response will strengthen your knowledge and allow you to tackle similar questions with confidence during the test.

Practice Tests for All Topics:

The book offers a number of practice examinations, each of which focuses on a distinct subject. This helps you to tailor your preparation and highlight areas that may need more inspection. Completing these practice exams will provide you with useful experience answering questions in a manner similar to the real exam.

Tips and Strategy:

Throughout the book, you will learn suggestions and tactics for improving your test-taking abilities. These ideas, which range from smart time management to strategies for dealing with difficult problems, can increase your confidence and performance on test day.

Realistic test simulation:

The practice exams are intended to closely approximate the circumstances of the real DMV Written Test. You'll be well-prepared to thrive in the test room if you're acquainted with the structure and sorts of questions you'll face.

TRAFFIC SIGNALS

Solid Red Light

A red traffic signal light indicates STOP. You may turn right at a red signal if:

- There is no NO TURN ON RED sign placed.
- Stop at the stop or limit line, yield to pedestrians, and turn when safe.

Red Arrow

A red arrow indicates STOP. Avoid turning at a red arrow. Stay halted until a green traffic signal light or arrow emerges.

Flashing Red Lights

A flashing red signal light indicates STOP. After halting, you may go when it is safe.

Solid Yellow Light

A yellow traffic signal light indicates CAUTION. The light is going to turn red. If you can safely stop at a yellow traffic light, do so. If you are unable to stop safely, go gently across the junction.

Yellow Arrow

A yellow arrow indicates that the protected turning time is about to finish. The signal will change shortly. If you are unable to stop safely or are already at the intersection, proceed gently with your turn. Pay attention for the following signal. This might be a:

- Green or red traffic light.
- Red arrow.

Flashing Yellow Light

A flashing yellow traffic light is a reminder to proceed with caution; slow down and be attentive. You do not have to quit.

Flashing Yellow Arrow

You may make a turn, however it is not shielded from other vehicles. Turn left after yielding to incoming traffic, and continue with care.

Solid Green Light

A green traffic light indicates GO. You must still stop for any car, bike, or pedestrian crossing the junction. Proceed only if there is adequate room to avoid endangering any incoming vehicles, bicyclists, or pedestrians. Do not enter the junction if you cannot cross entirely before the traffic light turns red.

Green Arrow

A green arrow indicates that you should go in the direction it points. The green arrow indicates a protected turn. A red traffic light causes oncoming cars to halt.

Traffic Lights Not Working

When a traffic signal malfunctions, halt as if the junction is controlled by halt signs in all directions. Then continue with caution when it is safe to do so.

Pedestrian Signals and Signs

WALK, Walking Person

You may cross the street.

Don't Walk or Raise Hand

You may not cross the street.

Flashing Don't Walk or Raised Hand

Don't start crossing the street. The traffic light is going to change. Drivers must yield to pedestrians, even if the Don't Walk signal is blinking.

Numbers

The numbers indicate how many seconds are remaining till you may cross the street.

Diagonal Crossing

These are crisscross and diagonal crosswalks, which enable people to cross the junction in either direction at once. Cross only when the walk signal permits it.

Sounds

Beeping, chirping, and spoken signals may aid blind or visually impaired individuals cross the roadway.

Pedestrian Push Button

This activates the Walk or Walking Person signal.

No pedestrian signals.

If there are no pedestrian lights, then follow the vehicle traffic signals.

Signs

Follow all warning signs, regardless of form or color.

STOP Sign

Make a complete stop before entering the crosswalk or approaching the limit line. If there is no limit line or crosswalk, come to a halt before approaching the crossing. Before going, be sure to check traffic in all directions.

Red YIELD Sign

Slow down and prepare to stop to let any car, bike, or pedestrian to pass before proceeding.

Red and White Regulatory Sign

Follow the sign's instructions. For example, DO NOT ENTER indicates do not enter the road or ramp where the sign is shown.

WRONG WAY Sign.

If you enter a highway against traffic, DO NOT ENTER and WRONG WAY signs may appear. When it is safe, back away or turn around. If the road reflectors flash red in your headlights when driving at night, you know you're headed the wrong way.

Red circle with a red line across it

The image within the circle depicts what you cannot accomplish and may be represented with words.

Yellow and Black Circular or X-shaped Sign

You are nearing a railroad crossing. Look, listen, slow down, and be prepared to halt. Allow any trains to pass before you continue.

Many railroad crossings contain a blue and white sign indicating what to do in the event of an emergency on or near the tracks, or if your car has stuck on the rails.

Five-sided sign

You're near a school. Drive gently and stop for youngsters in the crosswalk.

Diamond-shaped Sign

Alerts you to particular road conditions and risks ahead.

White Rectangular Sign

Communicates several vital regulations that you must follow.

Warning Signs

Warns about pedestrians, bikers, schools, playgrounds, school buses, and school passenger loading zones.

Red and White Regulatory Signs

No U-Turn   No Left Turn   No Right Turn

White Regulatory Signs

Highway Construction and Maintenance Signs

Guide Signs

Hazardous Loads Placards   Slow Moving Vehicle

Slippery
When Wet

Merging
Traffic

Divided
Highway

Two Way
Traffic

Lane Ends

End Divided
Highway

Traffic Signal
Ahead

Pedestrian
Crossing

Added Lane

Crossroad

Stop Ahead

Yield Ahead

Directional
Arrow

Curve

T
Intersection

Winding Road

Right of Way Rules: Who Goes First?

Right-of-way regulations clarify who goes first when automobiles, pedestrians, and bikes collide on the road. The car that arrives at the junction first has the right of way. Other drivers, bicycles, and pedestrians must wait for the individual with the right-of-way. Never assume other drivers will give you the right of way. Give up your right-of-way when it will assist avert a crash.

Intersections

Red and White Regulatory Signs

No U-Turn

No Left Turn

No Right Turn

White Regulatory Signs

Highway Construction and Maintenance Signs

Guide Signs

Hazardous Loads Placards

Slow Moving Vehicle

Warning Signs

Slippery When Wet	Merging Traffic	Divided Highway	Two Way Traffic
Lane Ends	End Divided Highway	Traffic Signal Ahead	Pedestrian Crossing
Added Lane	Crossroad	Stop Ahead	Yield Ahead
Directional Arrow	Curve	T Intersection	Winding Road

Right of Way Rules: Who Goes First?

Right-of-way regulations clarify who goes first when automobiles, pedestrians, and bikes collide on the road. The car that arrives at the junction first has the right of way. Other drivers, bicycles, and pedestrians must wait for the individual with the right-of-way. Never assume other drivers will give you the right of way. Give up your right-of-way when it will assist avert a crash.

Intersections

An intersection is any location where one road joins another. Controlled junctions have signs or traffic signals. Uncontrolled or blind junctions do not. Before approaching a junction, glance left, right, and ahead for cars, bicycles, and pedestrians. Be prepared to slow down and halt if needed. Pedestrians always have the right of way. Here are several right-of-way laws for intersections:

- Without STOP or YIELD signs, the vehicle that arrives first at the junction has the right of way. If a car, pedestrian, or bike arrives at the junction at the same moment as you, give the right of way to the one on your right. If you approach a stop sign and there are stop signs on all four corners, stop first and then continue as described above.
- T junctions without STOP or YIELD signs: Vehicles, bikers, and pedestrians on the through route (going straight) have the right of way.
- Turning left: Look for pedestrians. Give the right of way to any person or approaching vehicle that is dangerously near.
- Turning right: Keep an eye out for people crossing the street, as well as motorcyclists and bicycles going beside you.
- Green traffic light: Proceed with care. Pedestrians have the right of way.
- When entering traffic, you must continue with care and yield to existing vehicles in the lanes. It is illegal to halt or block an intersection when there is insufficient room to fully cross before the traffic light turns red.

Roundabouts

In a roundabout, traffic moves in a single direction around a center island.

How To Use A Roundabout:

1. Slow down as you approach.
2. Yield to all cars already on the circle.
3. When there is adequate space in traffic to merge safely, enter to the right.
4. Keep an eye out for directional signage and lane markers.
5. Travel in a counterclockwise direction. Don't stop or pass.
6. Signal while changing lanes or exiting.

7. If you miss your exit, go around until you find it again.

If the roundabout has many lanes, choose an entering or departure lane depending on your destination. This is shown in the figure below. To:

1. Turn right (yellow car): Select the right lane and depart in that lane.
2. Go straight (red car): Select either lane. Exit in the same lane you entered.
3. Turn left: Enter and drive until you reach the exit in the direction you want (blue vehicle).

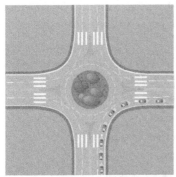

Right Turn

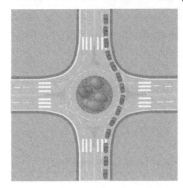

Straight

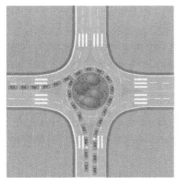

Left Turn

Pedestrians

These are considered pedestrians or vulnerable road users.

- A person walks.
- Someone who is not driving a car or riding a bicycle. This includes roller skates, skateboards, and so forth.
- A disabled person who uses a tricycle, quadricycle, or wheelchair to get about.

From left to right: tricycle, quadricycle, standard wheelchair, and electric wheelchair.

Pedestrians have the right of way, but they must also respect traffic regulations.

When a pedestrian crosses a street, whether or not there is a crosswalk, you must take care, slow down, or stop to enable the pedestrian to cross safely.

Additional considerations:

- Do not pass a car stopped at a crosswalk. You may not spot a person crossing the roadway.

- If a pedestrian establishes eye contact with you, they are prepared to cross the street. Yield to the pedestrian.
- Always give pedestrians adequate time to cross a roadway safely, since certain groups, such as elders, persons with young children, and people with disabilities, may need more time.

Crosswalks

A crosswalk is an area of the road designated for people to cross safely. They are often characterized with white lines. School crossings may feature yellow crosswalk markings. Not every crossing is marked.

Pedestrians have the right of way in crosswalks, whether marked or unmarked. If there is a limit line before the crosswalk, stop and let people cross the roadway.

Some crosswalks have flashing lights. Regardless of whether the lights are flashing, keep an eye out for pedestrians and ready to stop.

Pedestrians Who Are Blind

Pedestrians with guide dogs or white canes have the right of way at all times. These pedestrians are partly or completely blind. Be cautious while turning or backing up. This is especially crucial if you are driving a hybrid or electric car, since blind pedestrians depend on sound to detect a vehicle close.

- You should not stop in the middle of a crosswalk. This may cause a blind pedestrian to go into traffic outside of the crosswalk.
- Don't beep your horn at a blind person.
- When a blind person draws in their cane and walks away from the junction, it typically indicates that you can proceed.

Sharing The Road

Drivers must share the road with other cars, pedestrians, bikers, road crews, and huge vehicles.

Blind Spots (No Zone)

Drivers of large vehicles and trucks benefit from a greater vision in front of them as well as larger mirrors. They also have enormous blind patches, known as No Zones. In certain regions, your car may vanish from a big vehicle or truck driver's perspective. If you can't see the truck's side mirrors, the driver won't see you.

The shaded areas in this image are the truck driver's blind spots.

Braking

Larger vehicles and commercial trucks take longer to stop than passenger cars driving at the same speed. When traveling, they leave additional space in front of their car in case they need to stop unexpectedly. The typical passenger car moving at 55 mph can stop in 300 feet. A huge vehicle driving at the same speed may halt after up to 400 feet. The heavier the vehicle and the quicker it is driving, the longer it takes to properly stop; hence, a full truck will take longer to stop than an empty truck. Do not maneuver in front of a heavy car and abruptly slow or halt. The heavy car will be unable to stop quickly enough to avoid colliding with you.

Turning

When a vehicle rotates, the rear wheels travel a lesser distance than the front wheels. The length of the turning path varies proportionally with the length of the vehicle. This is why heavy cars and truck drivers must often swing wide to make a turn. When following a huge vehicle, check its turn signals before proceeding to pass. It seems to be turning one way, but it is really swinging wide in the other direction in order to turn.

Maneuvering

Larger cars and trucks are more difficult to manage than passenger automobiles. On a split highway with four or more traffic lanes in one direction, individuals may travel in the two lanes farthest to the right. When driving around heavy cars and trucks, do not:

- Change lanes right in front of them to go to an exit or turn.
- Drive next to them for longer than necessary. Always pass huge vehicles on the left side. After passing the massive car or truck, go ahead of it. Driving beside a huge truck makes it difficult for the driver to avoid hazards on the road.
- Follow too closely. Tailgating shortens a vehicle's safe distance.
- Underestimate their size and speed, since they often seem to be moving slowly.

Buses, Streetcars, and Trolleys

Safety zones are areas designated for pedestrians waiting for buses, streetcars, and trolleys. Raised buttons or markers are used to define safety zones on roadways. Never drive across a safety zone under any circumstances.

When a bus, streetcar, or trolley is stopped at a safety zone or traffic signal, you may pass at a maximum speed of 10 mph.

Safe Zones are marked by dotted white lines.

Do not overtake and pass a light rail vehicle or streetcar on the left side, whether it is moving or standing, unless:
Dotted white lines indicate safe zones.

Do not overtake or pass a light rail vehicle or streetcar on the left side, whether moving or stationary, unless:

- When the rails are too near to the right side for a passenger car to pass.
- You are on a one-way street.
- A traffic officer instructs you to pass on the left.

Light Rail vehicles

On public roadways, light rail cars have the same rights and obligations as other vehicles. To safely share the roadway with light rail vehicles:

- Be mindful of where they operate. Buildings, trees, and other things might create blind spots for the operator.
- Never turn in front of an oncoming light rail vehicle.
- Keep a safe distance.

- Before turning across the tracks, check for incoming light rail cars. Complete your turn only when the traffic signal indicates that you may go. Be careful that they have the potential to cause traffic signals to malfunction.
- Do not turn in front of a light rail vehicle.

Do not turn in front of light rail vehicles.

Motorcycles

Motorcycle riders have the same rights and obligations as other vehicles. To safely share the road with motorcycle riders:

- Check for motorbikes and utilize your mirrors while changing lanes or entering a road. Motorcycles are smaller in size and more difficult to discern, therefore they often vanish in car blind areas.
- Allow for a safe three-second following distance. This distance will assist you avoid colliding with a motorcycle if they abruptly halt or tumble.
- Whenever feasible, give a motorcyclist the whole lane. It is permitted to share lanes with motorbikes, sometimes known as lane splitting.
- Never attempt to pass a motorcyclist in the same lane as you.

- Before opening your door near to traffic, check for motorcycles.
- When feasible, shift to one side of your lane to allow motorcycle riders greater space to pass.

Motorcyclists may alter their speed or direction unexpectedly due to road conditions.

Emergency Vehicles

Give the right of way to any police enforcement, fire, ambulance, or other emergency vehicle equipped with a siren and red lights. Failure to pull over might result in a ticket. Drive to the right side of the road and stop until the emergency vehicle(s) has passed.

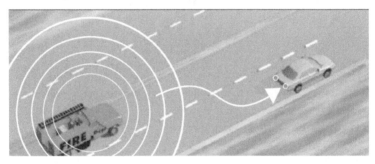

Yield to emergency vehicles.

When approaching a stopped emergency vehicle with flashing emergency signal lights (hazard lights), pull over and slow down.

If you are at an intersection and see an emergency vehicle, proceed through. As soon as it is safe, drive to the right and come to a halt.

Follow any guidance, command, or signal issued by a police officer or fireman. Follow their directions, even if they contradict existing signs, signals, or regulations.

Following within 300 feet behind a fire engine, police enforcement vehicle, ambulance, or other emergency vehicle with its siren or flashing lights turned on is against the law.

You may be arrested if you drive to the site of a fire, crash, or other tragedy. When you do this, you block the path of firemen, ambulance crews, and other rescue and emergency services.

Slow-moving vehicles

They may take longer to accelerate while entering traffic. Large trucks, bicycles, and certain vehicles slow down on long or steep slopes. Some slow-moving vehicles, such as road maintenance vehicles, have an orange and red triangle on the rear and typically move at 25 mph or less.

An example of a slow-moving vehicle.

Other sorts of slow-moving motorized vehicles that may operate on public roadways are:

- Scooters
- Neighborhood electric automobiles.
- Golf carts

Change your speed to share the road with these cars.

Neighborhood Electric Vehicles (NEV) and Low-Speed Vehicles (LSV)

Keep an eye out for slow-moving automobiles when you encounter these signs or markings:

- NEV USE ONLY.
- NEV ROUTE.

NEVs and LSVs can attain a maximum speed of 25 mph. They are not permitted to drive on roadways with speed limits above 35 mph.

Animal-drawn vehicles

Horse-drawn vehicles and individuals riding horses or other animals are permitted to use the road alongside motor vehicles. It is against the law to deliberately terrify horses or cattle.

Near Animals

If you notice a sign with an animal image, keep an eye out for animals on or near the road. If you observe animals or livestock on the road, slow down or stop and continue when it is safe. Make careful to follow the advice of the person in charge of the animals.

Bicycles

Bicyclists have the same rights and obligations as other drivers.

Cyclists may:

- Legally ride on some portions of highways if there is no other option and biking is not prohibited by law.
- Move to the left to escape dangers. These might be parked or moving cars, bicycles, animals, or rubbish.
- Choose to ride along the left curb or edge of a one-way street.
- You may utilize crosswalks by stopping and crossing like a pedestrian.

Bicyclists' responsibilities

As a biker, you must:

- Follow all traffic signs, signal lights, and fundamental right-of-way regulations.
- Ride in the same direction as traffic.
- Always check over your shoulder to ensure that the lane is free before turning or changing lanes.
- Yield to pedestrians.
- Wear a helmet (if you're under 18).
- Stay conspicuous (for example, never weave between parked cars).
- Ride as close to the right curb or edge of the road as possible.
- Do not ride on the sidewalk (unless permitted by the city).
- Make left and right turns using hand signals and turn lanes, much as a car would.
- Whenever feasible, utilize a bike lane or a through traffic lane.
- Have fully functioning brakes.

Examples of biker turns

Intersection with specific bike lanes.

Bicycling at Night

Bicyclists should avoid wearing dark clothes at night. Your bicycle must contain the following components:

- A front bulb emitting a white light viewable from 300 feet away.

- A built-in rear red reflector, as well as a solid or flashing red light. This must be visible at 500 feet.
- A white or yellow reflector placed on each pedal, the bicyclist's shoes, or their ankles. These must be visible from at least 200 feet.
- A white or yellow reflector on the front wheel, a white or red reflector on the back wheel, or reflective tires.

Bicycling on Travel Lanes

Bicyclists riding slower than the flow of traffic shall ride as near as practicable to the right curb or edge of the road, unless:

- Passing a car or a bicycle in the same direction.
- Preparing to take a left turn.
- Avoiding a danger or road situation.
- A lane is too small to safely accommodate both a bicycle and a car.
- Approaching a right turn.
- On a one-way street with two or more lanes. In this instance, a biker may ride along the road's left curb or edge.

Drivers should maintain a safe distance. When it is safe, the biker should shift to a position where automobiles may pass.

Passing a Bicycle

To safely pass a biker in the travel lane, you may need to change lanes. In this situation, pass safely and return to your regular lane. Leave some distance between your car and the bike.

 Right

 Wrong

Allow at least three feet between your car and a bike if you are unable to change lanes. If you cannot provide three feet of room, do not pass the cyclist. This will allow you to avoid placing the biker in risk. Remember to:

- Allow bikers ample room so that they are not compelled to enter parked automobiles or open their doors.
- Only merge toward the curb or into the bike lane if it is safe.
- Merge carefully behind a bike before making a turn.

- Enter a bike lane no more than 200 feet before making a turn.
- Look for bikers while changing lanes or entering traffic. They may be hiding in a vehicle's blind zones.
- Be cautious while approaching or overtaking a bike on a two-lane road.

Roadworkers and Work Zones

When there are workers, slow-moving equipment, or blocked lanes ahead, warning signs and message boards will appear.

Proceed with caution through the work zone by:

- Slowing down.
- Allowing more space between cars.
- Expect an abrupt slowdown or stoppage.
- Keep an eye out for cars who are changing lanes.
- Avoiding distractions.

Cones, drums, and other obstacles will help you navigate the work zone. Prepare to slow or halt for highway equipment. Merge as soon as it is safe, without crossing any cones or drums. Keep an eye out for cyclists if the lanes are narrow or the shoulder is blocked. Follow particular signs or instructions from professionals, such as flaggers.

Fines and Double-Fine Zones

Fines for driving offenses in a construction zone might reach $1,000 or more. Anyone convicted of assaulting a highway worker risks a $2,000 fine and up to a year in jail.

Certain roadways are designated as Safety Enhanced-Double Fine Zones. This is attributable to a rise in collision-related injuries and deaths. Fines are doubled in certain zones.

Fines are also increased in highway construction or maintenance areas when personnel are present.

Move Over and Slow Down.

Drivers must yield and slow down for emergency and roadwork vehicles. This includes:

Stationary emergency cars and tow trucks with flashing amber warning lights.

Stopped roadwork vehicles with emergency flashing or amber warning lights.

Vehicles carrying hazardous loads

A diamond-shaped sign on a truck indicates that the cargo may be harmful (gas, explosives, etc.). Vehicles with these signs must come to a complete stop before crossing railroad lines.

Examples of hazardous load placards.

Heavy Traffic or Bad Weather

When there is heavy traffic or inclement weather, you must drive more slowly. At the same time, you should avoid impeding regular and acceptable traffic flow by driving too slowly. If you travel faster or slower than the speed limit, you may face citation. When another motorist is close behind you and wants to go quicker, shift to the right. If you wish to travel slower than other drivers, stay in the right lane. For further information, see Choosing a Lane in Section 6.

Towing

Drive in the far-right lane or a lane designed for slower cars when:

- Tow a car or trailer.
- Drive a truck with at least three axles.

If no lanes are designated and there are four or more lanes in your direction, you may only use the two lanes closest to the right border of the road.

Around Children

All cars must stop for school buses.

The speed restriction is 25 mph within 500 feet of a school while students are outdoors or crossing the roadway. In certain school zones, the speed restriction may be as low as 15 mph. When near a school, check for:

- Bicycles alongside pedestrians.
- School safety patrols and crossing guards. Always heed their instructions.
- Stopped school busses and children from crossing the roadway.
- ➢ When some school buses approach a stop to let students off, they flash yellow lights. The yellow flashing lights signal you to slow down and prepare to halt.
- ➢ When the bus flashes red lights (at the top, front, and rear), you must stop in either direction until the children are safely across the street and the lights cease flashing. Stay halted when the red lights are flashing. If you fail to stop, you might be fined up to $1,000 and have your driving privileges terminated for a year.
- ➢ If the school bus is on the other side of a split or multilane roadway (two or more lanes in each direction), you are not required to stop.

Blind intersections

An junction is called blind if there are no stop signs at any of the corners.

If your vision is obscured, gradually go forward until you can see. The speed limit at a blind junction is 15 mph.

Alleys

An alley is a path that is little more than 25 feet wide and used to reach the back or side entrances of buildings or properties. You may enter or depart a driveway or alley by driving on or crossing a sidewalk. The speed limit in an alleyway is 15 mph.

Near Railroad or Light Rail Tracks.

The speed restriction is 15 mph within 100 feet of a railroad crossing, yet you can't see the rails for 400 feet in either direction. You may go faster than 15 mph if the crossing is regulated by gates, a warning signal, or a flagman. At a railroad or train crossing:

- Flashing red caution lights signify that you must stop and wait. Do not cross the train tracks until the red lights stop flashing, even if the gate lifts.
- When the crossing devices or a person informs you that a train is approaching, stop at least 15 feet from the closest track.
- Do not pass under or around lowering gates. If the gates are down and you don't see a train arriving, contact the designated railroad emergency toll-free number or 911.
- Stop, gaze, and listen. If you see a train approaching or hear a horn or bell, don't cross. Many crossings have numerous railroads. Look both ways and only cross when it is safe.
- Expect to see a train on any track, at any time, going in any direction.
- Never stop on a train track. Wait and do not advance if you do not have enough space to fully cross the tracks. If you are on the tracks, you risk being injured or killed.
- Keep an eye out for cars that need to come to a complete stop before crossing train lines. These vehicles include buses, school buses, and vehicles with a hazardous materials sticker.

Business or Residential Districts

The speed restriction is 25 mph, unless otherwise indicated.

CHAPTER 1: RULES OF THE ROAD

1.1 Traffic Lights and Signs

1.1.1 Understanding of Traffic Signal Colors

Traffic lights are essential for managing traffic flow and maintaining motorist and pedestrian safety. One of the most important components of traffic signals is the use of various colors to send particular messages to vehicles. Understanding the significance of each traffic light color is critical for safe and compliant driving.

Red Light:

A red traffic signal means that cars must come to a full stop. It is critical to keep still until the light turns green.

Action: Completely stop behind the stop line or before approaching the junction. Wait until the light turns to green before moving.

Green light:

A green traffic light indicates that cars may go through the junction or down the road.

Proceed with caution through the junction, constantly yielding to pedestrians and any other cars that may still be present.

Yellow light:

A yellow traffic light notifies cars that the signal is about to become red. It means that drivers should plan to stop safely if it is safe to do so.

Slow down and halt if it is safe to do so. When the light turns red, do not try to drive through the junction at high speed.

Understanding the basic meanings and behaviors connected with traffic light colors is critical for observing traffic rules and guaranteeing the safety of all road users. It is critical to approach junctions with care, obey signal changes swiftly, and be aware of the probable behaviors of other cars on the road.

Right Turn on Red: In California, unless otherwise marked, automobiles are permitted to make a right turn after stopping at a red light as long as there is no oncoming traffic or pedestrian traffic in the crosswalk.

Left Turn on Red: In certain cases, a left turn on red from one one-way street to another may be authorized. Always look for signs that indicate if such turns are permitted.

Drivers help to improve the general safety and efficiency of the road network by knowing and obeying the meaning of traffic signal colors. This information is useful not just for the California DMV Written Test, but also in regular driving situations.

1.1.2 Regulation Signs

Regulatory signs are an important part of the road signage system since they provide critical information regarding traffic laws and regulations. These signs are intended to provide particular instructions to all road users. Understanding the different regulation signals is critical for safe and legal driving. Here are some common kinds.

Stop sign:

Shape: Octagonal (eight-sided) with white lettering spelling "STOP".

Meaning: Drivers must come to a full stop at the stoplight or before approaching the junction. Proceed only when the path is clear.

Yield sign:

Shape: An equilateral triangle (three sides) with a crimson border and the word "YIELD" written in red.

Meaning: Drivers must slow down and give way to cars or pedestrians at intersections or merging points. Proceed cautiously.

Sign: Do not enter.

Square or rectangular with a white backdrop, a red circle, and a diagonal line.

Meaning: Access to the road or highway is forbidden. Drivers must not enter the defined area, which is often against the flow of traffic.

Wrong way sign:

Square or rectangular with a white backdrop, a red circle, and a diagonal line.

Meaning: It indicates that a motorist is going in the incorrect way. Drivers must turn around and return to the right road.

One-way sign:

Shape: Square or rectangular with a white arrow on a black backdrop.

Meaning: Traffic can only flow in one way. Drivers may not go in the other direction.

No U-Turn Sign:

The shape is square or rectangular, with a white backdrop and a red circle with a diagonal line through a U-turn arrow.

This means that U-turns are not permitted at the location indicated by the sign.

The speed limit sign:

Shape: Square or rectangular, with a white backdrop and black text showing the maximum speed.

Meaning: The maximum speed permitted on that specific route or highway under normal circumstances.

Understanding and following regulation signs is critical for preserving road safety and avoiding accidents. It is critical to be aware of these indicators, heed their directions, and change your driving behavior appropriately. This information is not only necessary for passing the California DMV Written Test, but also for encouraging safe and responsible driving practices on the road.

1.1.3 Warning signs

Warning signs are an essential component of road signage, alerting drivers to anticipated hazardous conditions, changes in road layout, or possible risks. Recognizing and comprehending warning signals is critical for maintaining safe driving habits and avoiding accidents. Listed below are some typical warning signs:

1. Curve Ahead Sign

- Shape: A yellow diamond-shaped symbol.

- Symbol: A curved arrow showing the direction of the next curve.

- Meaning: Informs vehicles of an upcoming bend in the road. Slow down and ready to change your steering properly.

2. Slippery When Wet Sign:

- Shape: A yellow diamond-shaped symbol.

- Symbol: Image of a slick road surface.

- Meaning: The road may become slippery under damp or rainy circumstances. Drivers should moderate their speed and proceed with care.

3. Pedestrian Crossing Signs:

- Shape: A yellow diamond-shaped symbol.

- Symbol: Illustration of a person crossing the street.

- Meaning: Notifies cars of the existence of a pedestrian crossing ahead. Be prepared to yield to pedestrians at specified crosswalks.

4. Deer Crossing Sign:

- Shape: A yellow diamond-shaped symbol.

- Symbol: The image of a deer.

- Meaning: Alerts drivers of the likelihood of a deer crossing the street. Use care, particularly in rural or forested regions.

5. Sign indicating an intersection ahead:

- Shape: A yellow diamond-shaped symbol.

- Symbol: A T-shaped junction.

- Meaning: Informs cars of an oncoming junction. Prepare to slow down, look for approaching traffic, and obey right-of-way restrictions.

6. Traffic Signal Ahead Sign

- Shape: A yellow diamond-shaped symbol.

- Symbol: An image of a traffic signal.

- Meaning: Informs drivers that a traffic light is approaching. Prepare to modify your speed and adhere to traffic control devices.

7. Road Work Ahead Sign

- Shape: An orange diamond-shaped symbol.

- Symbol: Worker and construction symbol.

- Meaning: This indicates that roadwork or construction is about to begin. Drivers should prepare for lane closures, limited speed zones, and construction-related dangers.

8. Crossroad Ahead Sign

- Shape: A yellow diamond-shaped symbol.

- Symbol: An intersection symbol.

- Meaning: Warns cars of an imminent junction with another route. Keep an eye out for cross-traffic.

Understanding warning signals is essential for responsible driving. These signs offer drivers with useful information about the road ahead, helping them to anticipate and respond to any risks. Drivers may help to ensure their own and others' safety on the road by paying careful attention to warning signs. Familiarity with warning signals is important not just for passing the California DMV Written Test, but also for encouraging prudent and cautious driving practices.

1.1.4 Guide Signs

Guide signs are an important part of the road signage system, informing drivers about destinations, routes, services, and other places of interest. These signs are intended to help vehicles navigate the road network and get to their destinations safely. Understanding guide signs is essential for route planning, making educated choices, and having a safe and efficient driving experience. Here are some typical kinds of guidance signs:

1. Route Signage:

- Shape: A variety of forms (e.g., shields or rectangles) labeled with numbers or letters.

- Meaning: State the route number or name of the road the motorist is currently on or approaching. Aids drivers in navigating diverse roads and freeways.

2. Interstate Signs

- Shape: Signs are blue shield-shaped with red, white, and blue patterns.

- Symbol: Interstate highway numbers.

- Meaning: Identifies the entry and departure sites of the Interstate Highway System, a network of high-speed freeways that connects major cities across the United States.

3. Guide Exit Signs:

- Shape Green background with white writing and symbols.

- Symbol: Indicates impending exits, along with information on amenities available at the exit (for example, petrol stations, restaurants, and hotel).

- Meaning: Assists drivers in arranging exits to particular destinations and services along the roadway.

4. Directional Signs:

- Shape: Green background with white writing and arrows.

- Symbol: Arrows pointing towards impending exits or destinations.

- Meaning: Provides drivers with navigational information to help them find particular routes, cities, and services.

5. Mileage Signs:

- Shape: A green background with white letters.

- Symbol: Shows the distance between forthcoming destinations and exits.

- Meaning: Informs drivers of the distance between certain cities, towns, or areas of interest along the route.

6. Service Signs:

- Shape: Blue background with white writing and emblem.

- Symbol: Icons for services such as petrol stations, restaurants, motels, hospitals, and rest spaces.

- Meaning: Indicates the availability of different services at approaching exits, enabling drivers to schedule rest breaks or refueling.

7. Signs of Recreational and Cultural Interest

- Shape: Brown background with white writing and emblem.

- Symbol: Icons for recreational and cultural destinations (e.g., parks, historical places).

- Meaning: Gives drivers information about local attractions so they may make educated choices regarding diversions or visits.

Understanding guide signs is critical for effective navigation and making educated judgments when driving. These signs make driving safer and more fun, particularly when traveling in unknown locations. Familiarity with guide signs is important not just for passing the California DMV Written Test, but also for encouraging prudent and effective route planning on the road.

1.2 Right of Way Regulations

1.2.1 Intersection and Crosswalk

Intersections and crosswalks are key sites where right-of-way laws must be followed to ensure traffic safety and efficiency. Every motorist should understand how junctions and crosswalks work. Here's a full explanation of the right-of-way laws at junctions and crosswalks:

1. Controlled Intersections:

- Traffic lights: Follow the traffic lights. Green signals indicate that you have the right of way to advance, yellow signals warn of an oncoming red light, and red signals necessitate a full stop.

- Turning Signals: Follow the designated turning signals. Left-turn arrows, right-turn arrows, and green arrows signal whether to surrender, turn, or move cautiously.

2. Uncontrolled Intersections:

- Four-Way Stops: At junctions without traffic lights, four-way stops work on a first-come, first-served basis. The first car to arrive gets the right of way. If two cars arrive at the same time, the vehicle on the right takes priority.

3. T-Intersections:

- Through Traffic: Cars on the through road have the right of way. Vehicles on the ending road must surrender and continue when it is safe.

4. Yielding and merging:

- Yielding When Merging: When merging into traffic from a yield sign, wait for a safe space before advancing.

- Always yield to pedestrians at crosswalks. Wait for them to cross the road entirely before going.

5. Pedestrian Crosswalks:

- At designated crosswalks, yield to pedestrians. Stop as needed to enable them to pass securely.

- Unmarked Crosswalks: Any junction with no marked crosswalks is deemed to have an unmarked crosswalk. Pedestrians maintain the right of way, and automobiles must yield.

6. Turning Right On Red:
- Stop and Yield: Before turning right on a red signal, stop completely and yield to approaching vehicles and pedestrians. Make sure it's safe to turn.

7. Left Turn:
- When making a left turn, yield to approaching traffic. Make the turn only if it is safe and there is no oncoming traffic.

8. Traffic Circles and Roundabouts
- When entering a roundabout, yield to cars that are already there. Wait until there is a safe space before entering.
- When leaving a roundabout, yield to pedestrians and bicycles. Signal your desire to leave.

9. Emergency Vehicles
- When emergency vehicles with lights and sirens approach, give the right of way by pulling over to the right side of the road and stopping.

Understanding and following right-of-way laws at crossroads and crosswalks is critical for avoiding accidents and guaranteeing the safety of both vehicles and pedestrians. The consistent use of these regulations improves the overall efficiency and harmony of traffic flow. Mastery of these standards is not only required for passing the California DMV Written Test, but also for responsible and safe driving on the road.

1.2.2 Four-way Stops

Four-way stops are junctions with stop signs on each approach, resulting in a regulated environment where numerous routes merge. Understanding the right-of-way laws at these crossings is critical for ensuring safe and orderly traffic movement. Here's a full analysis of the regulations and processes at four-way stops:

1. Arrival and Right of Way:

- The first car to arrive at the junction has right of way.

- If two or more cars arrive at the same time, the one on the right takes priority.

2. Stopped and Proceeding:

- Bring to a full stop at the stop line or before entering the junction.

- Give way to any vehicle that has stopped ahead of you.

3. Pedestrian Rights of Way:

- Pedestrians have the right of way at four-way stops.

- Before going, wait for pedestrians to have fully crossed the road.

4. Cyclist and Motorist:

- Cyclists must observe the same laws as automobiles at four-way stops.

- Give the right of way to any bicycle or motorist who arrives first or is already at the junction.

5. Left Turn and Right of Way:

- When two cars approach a four-way stop from different directions and want to turn left, they should both turn behind each other to prevent a possible collision.

6. Signals and communication:

- Use turn signals to convey your intentions.

- Make eye contact with other vehicles or pedestrians to ensure that you are communicating clearly about who has the right of way.

7. Uncontrolled Intersections:

- If the traffic lights at a four-way stop are not working or there are no signs, regard the junction as uncontrolled.

- The right-of-way rules for uncontrolled junctions apply, with the first vehicle or the one on the right taking precedence if many cars approach at the same time.

8. Patience and caution:

- Be patient and cautious at four-way stops, particularly during busy times.

- Be prepared to yield to other cars and check that the junction is clear before moving forward.

9. Emergency Vehicles

- When an emergency vehicle with lights and sirens approaches, give the right of way by driving over to the right side of the road and stopping. Once the emergency vehicle has passed, continue following the right-of-way laws.

Understanding the right-of-way laws at four-way stops is critical for avoiding traffic congestion and guaranteeing the safety of all road users. Drivers must approach these crossroads with a thorough awareness of the laws and a firm resolve to obey them consistently. Knowledge and adherence to these regulations help to improve traffic flow and provide a safer driving environment. This knowledge is not only necessary for passing the California DMV Written Test, but also for safe and successful driving habits on the road.

1.2.3 Yield and Merging

Yielding and merging are important parts of driving, particularly while maneuvering traffic, changing lanes, or merging into freeways. Understanding the right-of-way regulations related to yielding and merging is critical for safe and effective traffic movement. Here's a thorough investigation of these concepts:

1. Yielding at Intersections:

- When approaching a junction without traffic signals or signs, yield to cars in the intersection or approaching from the right.

- Yield to pedestrians at crosswalks and wait for them to cross before continuing.

2. Yielding to Emergency Vehicles:

- When emergency vehicles with lights and sirens approach, cede the right of way by driving over to the right side of the road and coming to a stop. Allow the emergency vehicle to pass safely.

3. Yielding on freeway on-ramps:

- When merging into a highway, cars on the on-ramp often defer to traffic already on the freeway.

- Accelerate to match highway traffic speeds and merge when there is a safe space.

4. Merging with Traffic:

- When changing lanes or merging into traffic, yield to cars in the lane you're about to enter.

- Use your turn signal to announce your desire to combine, and check your blind areas before making your move.

5. Lane Changes on the Freeway

- When changing lanes on a multi-lane expressway, slower traffic should yield to quicker traffic.

- Check your mirrors and blind zones before changing lanes.

6. The Zipper Merge:

- When merging lanes in heavy traffic, use the "zipper merge" strategy. Vehicles from each lane merge alternately into the fewer lanes.

- This strategy promotes smooth traffic flow and eliminates congestion.

7. Yielding to Bicycles

- When sharing the road with bicycles, yield to them when necessary, particularly at crossroads and curves.

- Keep a safe distance while passing bikers.

8. Regarding pedestrians:

- Always yield to pedestrians at crosswalks, crossings, and other marked pedestrian areas.

- Be cautious and patient, enabling pedestrians to finish their crossing.

9. Emergency lanes and service vehicles:

- Give way to emergency vehicles traveling in emergency lanes. Move to the right and clear a route for them.

- Yield to service vehicles, such as tow trucks or maintenance vehicles, and help damaged automobiles.

10. Being Predictable:

- Consistent and predictable driving style allows other drivers to anticipate your actions.

- Avoid sudden lane changes and provide enough of warning before yielding or merging.

Understanding and regularly implementing yielding and merging laws leads to safer roads and more harmonious traffic flow. Drivers who understand these right-of-way rules may confidently manage junctions and merging points, increasing overall road safety. Mastery of these ideas is not only required for passing the California DMV Written Test, but also for safe and defensive driving practices on the road.

1.3 Speed Limits and Safe Driving.

1.3.1 Speed Limitations

Understanding and sticking to speed limits is an essential component of responsible and safe driving. Speed restrictions are designed to improve road safety, decrease accidents, and promote a smooth traffic flow. Here's a thorough examination of speed limits and their relevance.

1. Basic Speed Law

- The Basic Speed Law mandates drivers to travel at a speed that is safe and acceptable given the current road, weather, and traffic circumstances.

- Drivers must always adapt their speed to fit the conditions, even if it is lower than the official speed limit.

2. Posted Speed Limits:

- Signs mounted on roads and highways indicate speed restrictions. These indications indicate the maximum permitted speed under ideal circumstances.

- Different speed restrictions may apply to different kinds of routes, such as residential neighborhoods, school zones, and highways.

3. School Zone:

- Reduced speed restrictions are often enforced in school zones during times when kids are coming or departing.

- These guidelines are intended to improve the safety of children crossing roadways and entering or departing school grounds.

4. Construction Zones:

- To protect both vehicles and workers, construction zones often have reduced speed restrictions.

- Speeding penalties in construction zones are often greater than ordinary fines.

5. Minimum speed limits:

- Some roads, particularly highways, may have minimum speed restrictions to maintain safe and continuous traffic flow.

- Driving drastically below the minimum speed limit may cause traffic congestion and raise safety concerns.

6. Variable speed limits:

- In certain regions, particularly on highways, variable speed restrictions may be in place depending on real-time traffic and weather conditions.

- Speed limits on electronic signs are changed in response to changing conditions.

7. Adverse Weather Conditions:

- Drivers are obliged to restrict their speed in unfavorable weather conditions such as rain, snow, or fog in order to maintain safe vehicle control.

- Inclement weather may make it more difficult to enforce speed restrictions, so drivers should proceed with care.

8. Speed limits for special vehicles:

- Specific vehicle classes, such as trucks, buses, and recreational vehicles, may have different speed limitations.

- These restrictions are often set to fit the handling qualities and braking capabilities of these vehicles.

9. Radar and Speed Cameras:

- To monitor and enforce speed restrictions, law enforcement may deploy radar or speed cameras.

- Fines or other penalties may be imposed in response to violations identified by these devices.

10. Driver Responsibilities:

- It is the duty of every motorist to be aware of and follow stated speed limits.

- Driving at a safe and appropriate pace improves overall road safety and helps to avoid accidents.

Understanding the subtleties of speed limits and constantly adhering to them is critical not just for passing the California DMV Written Test, but also for encouraging responsible and safe driving practices. Safe driving entails adapting speed to the surroundings and circumstances, therefore assuring the safety of all road users.

1.3.2 Adverse Weather Conditions

Adverse weather conditions provide particular problems for drivers, necessitating changes in driving habits to guarantee road safety. Understanding how various weather conditions affect driving and taking advised safeguards is critical. Here's a thorough examination of driving in poor weather conditions:

1. Rain:

- Reduced Visibility: Rain reduces visibility, necessitating the use of headlights and windshield wipers.

- Slippery Roads: When rainy, roads may become slippery; to avoid hydroplaning, lower speed and increase following distances.

2. Snow and Ice:

- Slippery Roads: Snow and ice may create dangerous driving conditions. Slow down and keep a safe distance from other cars.

- Traction Issues: To prevent skidding, carefully accelerate and decelerate. In regions where it snows heavily, use snow chains or winter tires.

3. Fog:

- Limited Visibility: Fog lowers visibility, so if you have low-beam headlights and fog lights, use them.

- Reduce Speed: Slow down and proceed with care. Avoid unexpected moves and be prepared for quick changes in visibility.

4. Wind:

- Vehicle Control: High winds may interfere with vehicle control, particularly for high-profile vehicles such as trucks and buses.

- Steering and Speed: Keep a firm hold on the steering wheel and lower speed to mitigate the impact of heavy crosswinds.

5. Thunderstorms:

- Reduced Visibility and Hydroplaning: Heavy rain during thunderstorms may impair visibility and increase the danger of hydroplaning. Reduce speed and utilize headlights.

- Lightning: If vision is significantly reduced, consider pulling over safely until circumstances improve.

6. Hail:

- Reduced Visibility: Hail may cause dangerous circumstances. Slow down, activate your vehicle's hazards, and pull over safely if needed.

- Potential Damage: Large hailstones might cause car damage. Seek refuge or park beneath a structure if feasible.

7. Extreme Heat

- Vehicle Maintenance: Excessive heat might impair your vehicle's performance. Maintain your car properly and check coolant levels on a regular basis.

- Hydration: Keep hydrated, particularly on lengthy rides in hot weather. To avoid heat-related diseases, take rests in shady places.

8. Freezing Rain:

- Ice Accumulation: Freezing rain may cause ice to form on highways and other surfaces. Drive with great care and consider postponing your trip if the weather is bad.

- Treat Surfaces as ice: Even if the roadways seem wet, they might be ice. Proceed with care and be ready for decreased traction.

9. Tornadoes:

- take refuge: If tornadoes are anticipated or witnessed, take refuge in a solid structure. Do not try to outrun a tornado in your car.

10. Flash Flooding:

- Avoid Flooded regions: Do not try to drive through flooded regions. Turn around and take a different way.

- Elevated Water Levels: Heavy rains may cause rapidly increasing water levels, presenting a serious danger.

The key in unfavorable weather circumstances is to prioritize safety. Adjust your driving habits, limit your speed, and be alert. It is important to be aware of weather predictions before going on a travel and to be prepared for shifting circumstances. Understanding how unfavorable weather impacts driving is essential not just for passing the California

DMV Written Test, but also for encouraging responsible and safe driving behaviors in real-world circumstances.

1.3.3 Proper Following Distances

Maintaining a safe following distance is an essential part of defensive driving and contributes considerably to road safety. The spacing between your car and the one in front of you is critical for avoiding accidents and giving you enough time to respond. Here's a full analysis on safe following distances:

1. The Three Second Rule:

- The "Three-Second Rule" is a basic guideline for following distances. Choose a stationary item on the road ahead, and when the car in front of you passes it, count "one thousand one, one thousand two, one thousand three." You should not approach the object until you complete counting.

- In inclement weather or while pulling a trailer, increase the following distance to six seconds or more.

2. Factors That Affect Following Distance:

- Speed: As the speed of the vehicle rises, so does the time required to respond and bring it to a halt. As a result, maintain a longer following distance at faster speeds.

- Weather circumstances: Adverse weather circumstances, such as rain, snow, or fog, need greater following distances to allow longer stopping distances.

- Vehicle Conditions: The condition of your vehicle, particularly the brakes and tires, might influence the stopping distance. To optimal performance, be sure to do routine maintenance.

3. Stopping distance:

- The stopping distance is calculated by adding the perception, response, and braking distances.

- Perception Distance: The distance traveled while identifying a danger.

- Reaction Distance: The distance traveled when shifting the foot from accelerator to brake.

- Braking Distance: The distance traveled after using the brakes to bring the vehicle to a full stop.

4. The Dangers of Tailgating

- Tailgating, or driving too closely, is a frequent cause of rear-end accidents.
- Tailgating shortens response time, increases the chance of a crash, and may cause a chain reaction if the car in front abruptly stops.

5. High Traffic and Stop-and-Go Conditions:

- Maintaining a reasonable following distance in heavy traffic or stop-and-go situations helps to avoid continuous braking and acceleration.
- It acts as a buffer, allowing you to respond to the speed variations of the cars ahead without putting too much strain on your brakes.

6. Large vehicles and trucks:

- When following big cars or trucks, be in mind that their rearview mirrors have restricted vision.
- Maintain a longer following distance to ensure that you are seen to the driver of the bigger car.

7. City Traffic and Intersections:

- When driving through cities and approaching junctions, give plenty of space between your car and the one in front of you.
- This enables for rapid repositioning if necessary and decreases the likelihood of a rear-end accident.

8. Anticipated Brake Lights:

- Keep an eye on the brake lights of the car in front of you and be prepared for stops or slowdowns.
- Anticipating variations in pace enables a smoother and more regulated reaction.

9. Highway Driving

- On highways, increase your following distance to allow for faster speeds and unforeseen traffic circumstances.
- Maintain a steady speed to avoid sudden stops or changes in speed.

10. Adapting To Traffic Conditions:

- Always adjust your following distance to the traffic around you.

- Use extra caution in congested areas, school zones, and construction zones, where unexpected stops are more likely.

Maintaining a safe following distance is a proactive measure that acts as a buffer for unexpected roadside events. Consistent adherence to safe following distances is critical not only for passing the California DMV Written Test, but also for promoting responsible and defensive driving practices in real-world driving scenarios.

CHAPTER 2: TRANSPORTATION LAWS AND REGULATIONS

2.1 California Vehicle Code Overview

The California Vehicle Code (CVC) is a comprehensive set of laws and regulations governing the use of vehicles on California roads. It covers a wide range of topics including driving, traffic laws, vehicle registration, safety equipment, and much more. To drive safely and legally, all drivers must understand the California Vehicle Code. Here's a summary of key aspects of the California Vehicle Code:

1. Traffic Laws:

- The CVC develops traffic laws, such as speed limits, right-of-way rules, and signaling requirements at intersections.

- It describes the legal requirements for stopping at stop signs and red lights, yielding to pedestrians, and other critical aspects of safe driving.

2. Driver Licenses:

- The CVC issues regulations governing driver's licenses, such as the application process, testing requirements, and restrictions for various types of licenses.

- It defines the penalties for driving without a valid license, as well as the consequences of license suspension or revocation.

3. Register your vehicle:

- The code describes the procedures for registering vehicles in California, including the necessary documentation, fees, and renewal processes.

- It addresses license plate, registration sticker, and vehicle ownership transfers.

4. Traffic Infractions and Penalties:

- The CVC lists various traffic violations and their corresponding penalties, such as fines, license points, and possible license suspension.

- It includes provisions for handling citations, traffic school options, and the consequences of accumulating too many points on a driver's license.

5. Vehicle equipment and safety standards:

- The code establishes specifications for vehicle equipment such as lighting, brakes, tires, and mirrors.

- It establishes vehicle safety standards to ensure that they meet specific roadworthiness requirements.

6. Rules for Specific Vehicle Types:

- The CVC contains regulations for specific types of vehicles, such as commercial vehicles, motorcycles, bicycles, and electric scooters.

- It specifies the safety requirements, licensing, and operational procedures for these vehicle categories.

7. Pedestrian Rights and Regulations:

- The code addresses pedestrian rights and responsibilities, including rules for using crosswalks, obeying traffic signals, and interacting with vehicles on the road.

8. Drug- and alcohol-related offenses:

- The CVC contains sections on driving under the influence (DUI) of alcohol or drugs.

- It establishes legal limits for blood alcohol concentration (BAC) and outlines the penalties for DUI offenses.

9. Accident Reporting and Insurance:

- The code specifies how to report traffic accidents and the requirements for maintaining auto insurance coverage.

- It outlines the responsibilities of drivers involved in accidents as well as the consequences of driving without insurance.

10. Other provisions:

- The CVC has a variety of measures that address a broad range of issues, such as the use of mobile phones while driving, carpool lane restrictions, and autonomous vehicle laws.

Understanding the California Vehicle Code is critical for all drivers seeking to comply with state rules and regulations. The code is often modified to reflect changes in traffic legislation and developing technology. Familiarity with the California Vehicle Code not only helps you pass the California DMV Written Test, but it's also crucial for encouraging safe, legal, and responsible driving behaviors on California's highways.

2.1.1 Key Sections of the California Vehicle Code

The California Vehicle Code (CVC) is a comprehensive legislative code that governs driving, vehicle operation, and traffic safety. Understanding major portions of the Vehicle Code is essential for all California drivers. Here's a full summary of some important sections:

1. Section 22348 - Speed Laws:

- This section explains the speed limitations for California roadways. It establishes maximum speed limits for several kinds of highways and includes heightened penalties for speeding infractions, particularly in construction zones.

2. Section 23123, Cell Phones and Driving:

- This clause forbids texting or chatting while driving and requires a hands-free device. It imposes penalties for infractions and emphasizes the necessity of reducing distractions for safer driving.

3. Section 21750 - Right of Way Rules:

- Establishes guidelines for right-of-way at junctions. It establishes standards for yielding, pausing, and moving in various traffic conditions, so promoting safe and orderly traffic flow.

4. Section 23152 - DUI (Driver Under the Influence):

- This section describes the regulations governing driving under the influence of alcohol or drugs. It discusses legal blood alcohol content (BAC) limits, DUI punishments, and repercussions such as license suspension.

5. Section 21650 - Keep Right and Minimum Speed Law

- Addresses the obligation for drivers to remain on the right side of the road, particularly on multi-lane roads. It also specifies minimum speed restrictions in some scenarios to promote traffic flow.

6. Section 21453: Traffic Signal Violations:

- Specifies the rules for respecting traffic signals such as red lights and green arrows. Violations may result in penalties, and the section underlines the significance of following signal instructions.

7. Section 21703 – Following Too Closely:

- Describes the guidelines for keeping a safe following distance. Tailgating is forbidden, and this section highlights the need of keeping a safe distance to avoid rear-end incidents.

8. Section 21200: Bicycle Regulations:

- Describes bikers' rights and obligations on California highways. It includes restrictions for riding on streets, bike lanes, and helmets, all of which promote safe coexistence with motor vehicles.

9. Section 22500: Parking Regulations

- Addresses parking rules and restrictions. It addresses restricted parking zones, time limitations, and disabled parking, as well as offering guidance for acceptable and polite parking practices.

10. Section 21754 - Passing to the Right:

- Establishes guidelines for transferring the right, stressing that it should only be done in certain situations. This part helps to ensure safe overtaking techniques and traffic flow.

11. Section 21655 - Carpool Lane Violations

- Describes the guidelines for utilizing carpool (HOV) lanes. It specifies the minimum number of people, the permitted entrance and departure locations, and the repercussions of breaking carpool lane rules.

12. Section 21710 - Obstruction of Traffic

- Addresses the restriction on hindering traffic by driving at slower speeds or blocking the usual flow of cars. This section highlights the need to maintain a moderate and safe speed.

13. Section 21760: Bicycle Lanes

- Establishes standards for how bikers and vehicles should utilize bicycle lanes. It specifies guidelines for the safety and shared use of dedicated bike lanes.

14. Section 22517 - Disabled Parking

- Outlines restrictions governing handicapped parking places, such as the display of disability placards or license plates. This section underlines the necessity of respecting disabled parking places.

15. Section 22450 - Stop Sign Violations:

- Establishes guidelines for halting at stop signs. This section describes the necessity to come to a full stop, cede the right of way, and move safely, which helps to improve junction safety.

Understanding these important provisions of the California Vehicle Code is critical for all drivers. It not only helps you pass the California DMV Written Test, but it also encourages careful and legal driving, which contributes to overall road safety.

2.1.2 Legal Implications of Violations

Violating the California Vehicle Code (CVC) may result in a variety of legal penalties. Understanding the repercussions is critical for all drivers in order to encourage safe and responsible driving behaviors. Here's a full summary of the legal implications connected with infractions of the California Vehicle Code:

1. Fines:

- One of the most typical penalties for breaking traffic regulations is the imposing of fines. The sum varies according on the kind and severity of the offense.

- Traffic penalties may vary from small violations like incorrect parking to more significant crimes like speeding or running red lights.

2. Traffic School:

- For some traffic infractions, the court may provide the opportunity to attend traffic school. Individuals who complete an accredited traffic school course may avoid having the ticket recorded on their driving record.

- Attending traffic school is a common technique to have a clean driving record and prevent increases in insurance premiums.

3. License Points:

- Violations of the California Vehicle Code may result in the issuance of points on a driver's record. Points are allocated depending on the seriousness of the violation.

- Accumulating too many points in a given time period may result in further sanctions, such as license suspension or the necessity to attend a driving development program.

4. License Suspension/Revocation:

- Serious infractions, numerous traffic crimes, or an excessive number of points on a driving record may result in the suspension or revocation of a driver's license.

- License suspension terms vary based on the severity of the infractions, and restoration often requires meeting certain conditions, such as serving the suspension time or attending driver development programs.

5. Higher Insurance Premiums:

- Insurance companies may boost prices for drivers who have a history of traffic offenses or accidents. The severity and frequency of offenses influence the effect on insurance prices.

- Keeping a clean driving record is critical for obtaining lower insurance costs.

6. Probation:

- Probation may be imposed by a court as part of the punishment for certain traffic violations. Individuals on probation are required to follow certain requirements, such as attending therapy or refraining from subsequent infractions.

- Failure to comply with probationary conditions may result in more severe repercussions.

7. Community Service

- Courts may require people convicted of traffic violations to undertake community service as part of their punishment. Community service enables people to give back to their communities while also completing their legal requirements.

8. Vehicle Impoundment:

- Authorities may confiscate a person's car for specified infractions such as driving with a suspended license or driving while intoxicated. Vehicle impoundment adds another level of punishment to some significant offenses.

9. Criminal Charges:

- Some traffic offenses, especially those involving reckless driving, DUI, or hit-and-run accidents, may result in criminal prosecution.

- Criminal charges may result in more serious legal penalties, such as fines, probation, and perhaps jail.

10. Warrants and arrests:

- Ignoring traffic tickets or failing to appear in court as scheduled may result in the issue of arrest warrants. People who have outstanding warrants may be arrested by law authorities.

Understanding the possible legal penalties of breaching the California Vehicle Code emphasizes the significance of driving responsibly and legally. Staying knowledgeable about traffic rules, adopting safe driving practices, and following regulations are critical for avoiding these penalties and helping to overall road safety. Knowledge of these repercussions is not only necessary for passing the California DMV Written Test, but also for safe and defensive driving on the road.

2.2 Driving Under the Influence (DUI)

2.2.1 Blood Alcohol Concentration (BAC) Limits

Blood alcohol concentration (BAC) is a measurement of the quantity of alcohol in a person's bloodstream. It is an important metric for identifying a driver's degree of impairment from alcohol use. Specific BAC limits are set in California, as well as in many other jurisdictions, to determine permissible and prohibited blood alcohol concentrations. Knowing these restrictions is critical for all drivers. Here is a full review of the BAC limits in California:

1. Legal BAC Limits:

- In California, the normal legal blood alcohol concentration limit for drivers 21 and older is 0.08%. This implies that if a driver's BAC is 0.08% or greater, they are regarded to be driving under the influence (DUI).

- Commercial drivers, such as those holding a commercial driver's license (CDL), have a reduced legal limit of 0.04%. Commercial drivers have tighter requirements owing to the extra responsibilities and possible hazards connected with driving big or dangerous trucks.

2. Zero tolerance for underage drivers:

- California has a "Zero Tolerance" policy for drivers under the age of twenty-one. Individuals in this age range are prohibited from having any detectable alcohol in their system. Even BACs below 0.08% might result in sanctions, such as license suspension.

3. Increased Penalties for High BAC Levels

- While a basic DUI offense has a legal limit of 0.08%, those with greater BAC levels may face increased penalties. In California, greater BAC values, known as "High BAC" or "Excessive BAC," may result in heavier penalties, lengthier license suspensions, and required participation in alcohol education programs.

4. Impeded Consent Law:

- California has a legislation requiring implied consent. Individuals who get a driver's license implicitly agree to chemical testing if detained on suspicion of DUI. Refusing to take a breathalyzer or blood test may result in an immediate license suspension and additional consequences.

5. Factors that Influence BAC:

- BAC is affected by a variety of parameters, including the number of drinks drank, the kind of alcohol, body weight, metabolism, and the amount of time since drinking. It is important to note that people may react differently to the same quantity of alcohol depending on certain circumstances.

6. Breathalyzer and Blood Test:

- Breathalyzer or blood tests are often used by law enforcement to determine blood alcohol content. Breathalyzer testing offer quick findings, however blood tests may be performed at a medical institution. Both approaches are reliable for assessing blood alcohol concentration.

7. Field sobriety tests:

- Law enforcement uses field sobriety tests, such as the walk-and-turn or one-leg stand, to determine a driver's degree of impairment. While these tests aid in the determination of probable cause for a DUI arrest, they do not directly detect blood alcohol concentration.

8. The Effects of Exceeding BAC Limits:

- Exceeding the legal BAC limit may result in a variety of penalties, including fines, license suspension, required DUI education programs, probation, and even incarceration. Repeat violations and higher BAC levels result in more severe punishments.

9. Ignition Interlock Device (IID):

- People convicted of DUI may be obliged to install Ignition Interlock Devices (IIDs) in their cars. IIDs require drivers to produce a breath sample before starting the car, which prevents operation if alcohol is detected.

Understanding and adhering to BAC limits is critical for all drivers to guarantee responsible and safe driving. Avoiding intoxicated driving not only avoids legal implications, but it also improves overall road safety. Knowledge of BAC limits is essential not just for passing the California DMV Written Test, but also for encouraging safe and defensive driving practices on the road.

2.2.2 Punishments for DUI Offenses

In California, driving under the influence (DUI) violations carry a variety of punishments, the severity of which is determined by criteria such as past convictions, blood alcohol concentration (BAC) levels, and the existence of aggravating circumstances. Understanding the possible repercussions of DUI crimes is critical for all motorists. Here's a thorough breakdown of the consequences for DUI charges in California:

1. First Time DUI Offense:

For a first-time DUI offense in California with a BAC level of 0.08% or higher, penalties may include:

- Fines: Fines may vary from hundreds to thousands of dollars.

- License Suspension: A first infraction usually results in a six-month license suspension.

- DUI School: Completing a court-approved DUI education program is mandatory.

- Probation: A term during which certain criteria must be met.

- Possible Jail Time: In certain situations, a brief jail term may be issued.

2. Increased Penalties for High BAC Levels

- Higher BAC readings, sometimes referred to as "High BAC" or "Excessive BAC," may result in harsher penalties such as higher fines, lengthier license suspensions, and required participation in prolonged DUI education programs.

3. Second DUI Offense

- For a second DUI violation within ten years of a previous conviction, the penalties may include:

- Increased Fines: Fines are higher than those for a first offense.

- Extended License Suspension: A license suspension for up to two years.

- Installation of an Ignition Interlock Device (IID) is mandatory.

- DUI School: Completing an extensive DUI education program.

- Probation: A probationary term with stricter requirements.

- Possible Jail Time: Longer jail penalties than a first offense.

4. Third DUI Offense

- A third DUI violation within ten years of previous convictions is considered a more severe crime and may result in:

- Substantial Fines: Fines are higher than in past violations.

- Long-term License Revocation: The driver's license is revoked for up to three years.

- Mandatory IID: An IID must be installed.

- Long DUI School: Completion of an extensive DUI education curriculum.

- Felony Charges: In certain cases, a third DUI conviction may be prosecuted as a felony, resulting in more serious repercussions.

5. Extreme Situations:

- DUI crimes with aggravating circumstances, such as causing harm or death, may result in more severe consequences, such as felony charges, large fines, extended incarceration, and a possible strike on the individual's criminal record.

6. Driver License Suspension or Revocation:

- DUI convictions result in an automatic suspension or revocation of the driver's license. Individuals may be eligible for a limited license or must install an Ignition Interlock Device (IID) in order to restore driving privileges.

7. Ignition Interlock Device (IID):

- IIDs are often needed for DUI offenders, particularly for second and subsequent convictions. The gadget compels drivers to produce a breath sample before starting the car and at regular intervals while driving.

8. Probation:

- Probation is a typical component of DUI sentences. It entails adhering to particular restrictions, such as refraining from drinking, seeking therapy, and avoiding additional legal troubles.

9. DUI Expungement

- In certain situations, persons convicted of DUI may be eligible for expungement, which removes the conviction from their criminal record. Eligibility requirements and processes differ, and legal counsel is needed.

10. Insurance Premiums Increase

- DUI convictions can result in large increases in vehicle insurance prices. DUI charges are seen by insurance companies as high-risk conduct, leading in higher premiums for those who have been convicted.

Understanding the possible consequences for DUI convictions is critical for all drivers in order to make sound judgments regarding responsible and safe driving. The serious penalties of DUI convictions emphasize the necessity of avoiding intoxicated driving for individual well-being and community safety. Knowledge of DUI consequences is essential not just for passing the California DMV Written Test, but also for encouraging safe and defensive driving behaviors on the road.

2.3 Specific Driving Situations

2.3.1 School Zones

School zones are designated locations near educational institutions where extra safety precautions and lower speed restrictions are in place to protect kids, walkers, and cars. When entering or driving through a school zone, drivers must be aware of and follow special restrictions. Here is a full breakdown of school zones.

1. Lowered Speed Limits:

- School zones normally have lower speed restrictions during particular hours, usually at the beginning and end of the school day. The typical speed restriction in school zones is 15 or 25 mph, however the specific limit may vary.

- Slower speed restrictions are enforced to improve safety and give drivers more time to respond to possible risks, particularly in places where children may be present.

2. School Zone Signs and Markings

- School zones are identified by specific signs and road markings. Look for signs marking the beginning and conclusion of the school zone, as well as speed restriction signs.

- Road markings, such as crosswalks and school zone pavement markings, act as visual signals to warn vehicles to the existence of a school zone.

3. Flashing Beacons:

- Some school zones include flashing beacons or signs that activate at certain times to indicate that a lower speed restriction is in place.

- When the beacons flash, drivers must pay attention to them and modify their speeds appropriately.

4. School Crossing Guard:

- School crossing guards are responsible for assisting pedestrians, particularly kids, in safely crossing the road. Drivers must follow crossing guards' orders and give pedestrians the right of way at crosswalks.

- Crossing guards often utilize stop signs and hand signals to manage traffic and guarantee safe crossings.

5. Watch for pedestrians:

- Be extremely cautious in school zones, and keep an eye out for pedestrians, particularly youngsters. Children are not always aware of driving regulations, thus drivers must anticipate their actions.

- Be prepared to come to a rapid halt if a pedestrian enters the road, and always yield to those in crosswalks.

6. No passing:

- Passing other cars in school zones may be forbidden, particularly if the speed limit is decreased. Follow traffic restrictions and avoid passing other cars in certain places.

- No passing zones are used to provide a smooth and regulated flow of traffic, lowering the likelihood of an accident.

7. Avoid Distractions:

- Avoid distractions while driving through school zones. Avoid using your phone, changing the radio, or indulging in any other activity that takes your concentration away from driving.

- Maintaining concentration allows drivers to react swiftly to changing circumstances and unexpected situations in school zones.

8. Be Aware of School Buses:

- School buses often run in conjunction with school zones. Be mindful of the presence of school buses, particularly while they are stopped to pick up or drop off pupils.

- Follow school bus-related traffic rules, such as halting when the bus stretches its stop sign and flashing red lights.

9. Strict Enforcement

- Law enforcement officers often severely enforce driving laws in school zones to guarantee everyone's safety. Fines and penalties may be imposed for violating speed limits or other laws in certain places.

10. Adjust Driving Behavior

- Recognize the significance of modifying driving behavior in school zones. The protection of children and pedestrians is critical, and drivers play an important role in ensuring a safe environment.

All drivers must understand and follow school zone-specific restrictions. It helps to ensure the general safety of students, pedestrians, and automobiles in and around educational institutions. Understanding school zone restrictions is critical for passing the California DMV Written Test and instilling appropriate and defensive driving habits on the roads.

2.3.2 Railroad Crossing

Railroad crossings provide unique problems to vehicles, necessitating special procedures to guarantee safety and avoid train accidents. Understanding the laws and procedures for approaching and negotiating railroad crossings is critical for all motorists. Here is a complete review of train crossings.

1. Stop, Look, and Listen.

- When approaching a railroad crossing, automobiles should come to a full stop if the crossing gates are down, signals are activated, or warning lights are blinking.
- Come to a safe stop away from the tracks, leaving enough clearance for the full car to clear them.

2. Check For Trains:

- Before crossing the railroad lines, vehicles must visually inspect for incoming trains in both directions. Keep an ear out for train noises, particularly in low-light situations.
- Trains travel swiftly, and their size and speed may cause visual illusions. Never assume there is enough time to cross without doing a thorough inspection.

3. Look For Multiple Tracks:

- Some railroad crossings have numerous tracks. Prior to crossing, make sure that all tracks are clear. Wait until there is adequate room on the opposite side of the tracks to avoid being stopped in a wait when crossing.

4. Follow Warning Signs and Signals:

- Railroad crossings are marked with warning signs, signals, and gates. Follow all posted signs and signals, such as stop signs, crosswalks, and flashing lights.
- Do not try to cross the tracks until the warning lights are turned off, the gates have been lifted, and it is safe to continue.

5. No passing near railroad crossings:

- Never pass another vehicle at or near a railroad crossing. Passing through these regions is hazardous and may result in crashes with incoming trains.
- Follow traffic restrictions that prevent passing near train crossings.

6. Be careful at unguarded crossings:

- Some railroad crossings may lack operational warning lights and gates. Use additional care at unprotected crossings and be prepared to halt if required.

- Look for crossbuck signs that signal a railroad crossing. Treat each crossing as if a train is about to arrive.

7. Be aware of quiet trains:

- Trains may approach silently, particularly at slower speeds or when wind conditions obscure the sound. Even if you don't hear a train coming, be alert and depend on visual cues.

8. Watch for pedestrians and bicyclists:

- Railroad crossings are not only for automobiles; pedestrians and bikes may also utilize them. When approaching railroad crossings, be careful and give pedestrians and bicycles the right of way.

9. Stay Off Tracks

- Never stop or park on a train track. If a vehicle stalls or gets stopped on the rails, escape quickly and move away. If you want help, please call.

10. Proceed with Caution After a Train Passes

- After a train has passed, wait for the warning lights to turn off and make sure there are no further trains coming from either direction before going.

11. Take Extra Caution at Night:

- Nighttime railroad crossings might be more difficult to manage. To guarantee visibility and safety, proceed with care, utilize headlights, and pay attention to warning signs.

12. Follow state laws:

- Become familiar with state-specific train crossing rules. Different states' laws and regulations may differ, thus it is critical to understand local needs.

13. Report Malfunctions.

- If you see a faulty or damaged railroad crossing signal, gate, or lights, notify local authorities or the train operator right once. Malfunctions may offer major safety hazards.

Following safety requirements and being cautious at railroad crossings is critical for avoiding accidents and maintaining the safety of both vehicles and train passengers. Knowledge of railroad crossing laws is not only required to pass the California DMV Written Test, but it is also necessary to promote safe and defensive driving behaviors on the roads.

2.3.3 Emergency Vehicle

When encountering an emergency vehicle while driving, motorists must respond quickly and carefully to protect everyone's safety on the road. Emergency vehicles include police cars, ambulances, fire engines, and other law enforcement and emergency service vehicles. Here's a thorough breakdown of how drivers should engage with emergency vehicles:

1. Please yield the right of way:

- When an emergency vehicle approaches with flashing lights and sirens, cars must give the right of way. Move to the right side of the road and, if required, stop completely.

- Yielding immediately enables emergency vehicles to pass and arrive at their location without undue delays.

2. Pull Over Safely

- Pull over carefully for an emergency vehicle, and avoid halting at intersections or obstructing crosswalks. Allow adequate room for the emergency vehicle to pass through safely.

- If you are in heavy traffic and are unable to pull over right away, establish a clear route by expressing your desire to move aside.

3. Do not follow too closely.

- Avoid following emergency vehicles closely. Maintain a safe distance so that the emergency vehicle may make unexpected stops or movements.

- To effectively handle traffic, emergency vehicles may shift lanes or make unexpected moves.

4. Follow traffic signals and signs:

- Follow traffic signals and signs even while yielding to an emergency vehicle. Do not enter intersections on a red light or do dangerous maneuvers.

- Follow traffic control device directions to keep the road safe and orderly.

5. Stay away from intersections:

- If an emergency vehicle approaches a junction, do not enter, even if you have the right of way. Allow the emergency vehicle to pass safely before moving forward.

- Clear intersections allow emergency vehicles to proceed quickly while avoiding accidents.

6. Be Careful When Re-entering Traffic:

- After an emergency vehicle has passed, look for further emergency vehicles and proceed with caution back into traffic. Be advised that many emergency vehicles may be sent to the same occurrence.

7. Be Aware of Emergency Personnel:

- Emergency vehicles may convey both equipment and persons who may need to depart the vehicle at the site of an event.

- Allow emergency responders ample room to execute their jobs without jeopardizing their or others' safety.

8. Understanding Different Siren Sounds:

- Emergency vehicles may indicate their intentions using a variety of siren sounds. Learn the unique sounds of police sirens, ambulance sirens, and fire truck sirens so that you can respond effectively.

9. Adherence to Move Over Laws:

- Some states have "Move Over" rules, which mandate drivers to shift to another lane or lower speed when approaching stationary emergency vehicles with flashing lights.

- Understand and follow Move Over rules in your region to improve the safety of emergency workers operating on the side of the road.

10. Avoid Obstructing Emergency Vehicles:

- Do not impede the route of emergency vehicles or try to pass them. Such activities may hamper their growth and reduce their capacity to react to situations.

11. Caution in Construction Zones:

- Be especially cautious when approaching emergency vehicles in construction zones. Follow established speed restrictions and stay alert of shifting traffic patterns.

12. Stay informed about local regulations:

- Familiarize yourself with local rules governing contacts with emergency vehicles. Laws differ by jurisdiction, thus remaining up to date ensures that relevant requirements are followed.

Interacting appropriately with emergency vehicles is an essential component of defensive driving. By surrendering the right of way and according to established norms, drivers assist to improve the efficiency of emergency responses and preserve a safe driving environment. Knowledge of these rules is not only required for passing the California DMV Written Test, but it is also critical for encouraging responsible driving behaviors and protecting the safety of all drivers.

CHAPTER THREE: DEFENSIVE DRIVING

3.1 Defensive Driving Principles:

3.1.1 Predicting Hazards

Anticipating risks is an important ability for safe and defensive driving. It entails constantly monitoring the route, recognizing possible hazards, and taking proactive steps to prevent or lessen risks. Drivers who anticipate risks may make educated judgments and respond quickly to safeguard the safety of themselves, their passengers, and others on the road. Here's a comprehensive guide on predicting risks when driving:

1. VISUAL SCANNING:

- Effective hazard anticipation starts with a constant and methodical visual scan of the road ahead and the surrounding surroundings. Drivers should not focus on a single location, but instead scan their whole range of view.

- Check your rearview and side mirrors on a regular basis to be aware of cars coming from behind or in neighboring lanes.

2. Road conditions:

- Evaluate current road conditions, such as surface quality, the presence of barriers, and the signs. Consider possible dangers such as potholes, debris, or uneven terrain that might impair vehicle control.

3. Weather Condition:

- Consider the weather and how it may affect driving. Rain, snow, fog, or ice may cause slippery conditions and limit visibility. Adjust your driving speed and keep a safe following distance.

4. Traffic Flow:

- Be prepared for changes in traffic flow, such as congestion, unexpected halt, or unpredictable driving by other drivers. Pay attention to the brake lights and turn signals of cars ahead to anticipate changes in speed or direction.

5. Intersection Awareness:

- Be especially mindful of crossroads. Predict the behavior of other drivers, particularly those coming from various directions. Look for pedestrians, bicycles, and possible cross-traffic.

6. Pedestrians and cyclists:

- Be cautious of pedestrians and bicycles, especially in metropolitan regions, school zones, and residential neighborhoods. Prepare for probable crossings and give precedence to vulnerable road users.

7. Vehicle Movement:

- Plan for the movement of automobiles around you. Be cautious of merging traffic, lane changes, and driving behavior in neighboring lanes. Predictive driving enables prompt answers to possible conflicts.

8. Use of turn signals:

- Pay attention to the turn signals of other vehicles. Anticipate lane shifts and turns depending on signals, enabling you to alter your own driving to maintain a safe distance.

9. Construction Zones:

- Approach construction zones with care, anticipating changes in traffic patterns, decreased speed restrictions, and the presence of construction equipment or personnel. Follow stated signs and be ready for unforeseen situations.

10. The presence of animals:

- Keep an eye out for animals crossing roads in rural or forested areas. Anticipate the presence of animals and alter your pace to lessen your chances of colliding.

11. Potential Blindspots:

- Be aware of any possible blind spots in your car and other vehicles on the road. Before changing lanes, check your blind areas using a mirror and do a shoulder check.

12. Emergency Vehicles

- Be prepared for the presence of emergency vehicles, particularly while approaching a junction. Be prepared to surrender the right of way to emergency vehicles with active lights and sirens.

13. Distracted Driver:

- Be wary of distracted drivers using cell phones, navigation systems, or other devices. Anticipate unpredictable behaviour and keep a safe distance from such cars.

14. Preserve Escape Routes:

- Always leave adequate distance between your car and others to provide for an escape path. Anticipate possible risks by situating your car so that you have the ability to safely move if required.

15. Plan Ahead:

- Plan your journey in advance, taking into account probable risks and alternative routes. Being aware of road conditions, construction, and traffic patterns allows you to make educated judgments.

Drivers may improve their capacity to react successfully to changing road conditions if they actively anticipate potential risks. This proactive strategy improves overall road safety by lowering the chance of accidents. Knowledge of hazard anticipation is essential not just for passing the California DMV Written Test, but also for fostering prudent and cautious driving practices.

3.1.2 Maintaining Awareness

Maintaining awareness when driving is an essential part of safe and responsible vehicle operating. It entails being alert to your surroundings, monitoring road conditions, and being mindful of the behaviors of other road users. A cautious and observant driver is better able to foresee possible risks, make educated judgments, and react quickly to changing conditions. Here's a full description of being attentive when driving:

1. Remain Focused:
- Concentrate on driving and avoid distractions. Maintain focus on the road, other cars, and the surrounding surroundings. Distractions, such as using a cell phone, eating, or changing the radio, may reduce alertness.

2. Regular Visual Scanning:
- Always scan the road ahead, check rearview mirrors, and watch side mirrors to be aware of your surroundings. Regular visual scanning offers information about traffic conditions, possible risks, and other drivers' behavior.

3. Check your blind spots:
- Before changing lanes or completing a turn, do shoulder checks and utilize mirrors to look for blind spots. Being mindful of blind spots reduces the danger of colliding with cars that are not in your immediate range of view.

4. How to Use Mirrors:
- Make the most use of your rearview and side mirrors. Adjust them to improve visibility and reduce the possibility of blind spots. Check your mirrors on a regular basis to be aware of the locations of cars behind and alongside your vehicle.

5. Keep a safe following distance:
- Maintain a safe following distance to the car in front of you. This allows enough time to respond to unexpected halt or changes in traffic circumstances. The three-second rule is a basic guideline for ensuring a safe following distance.

6. Be Alert to Traffic Signs and Signals:

14. Limit Distractions:

- Reduce distractions inside the car. Avoid distractions while driving, such as texting, eating, or having extended discussions. To be alert, keep your eyes on the road.

15. Be Calm and Patient:

- Keep a calm and tolerant temperament while driving. Aggressive driving may reduce attentiveness and raise the likelihood of an accident. Allow ample time to get at your location without hurrying.

Maintaining awareness is an ongoing, proactive endeavor that leads to safe and responsible driving. A alert driver who keeps focused on the road and aware of their surroundings is better prepared to deal with changing driving conditions and possible threats. Maintaining attentiveness is not only necessary for passing the California DMV Written Test, but also for developing safe and defensive driving behaviors.

- Pay attention to traffic signs, lights, and pavement markings. Awareness of traffic control devices aids in comprehending road laws, forthcoming crossroads, and speed limit adjustments.

7. Respect Speed Limits:

- Follow stated speed restrictions. Maintaining awareness of speed restrictions helps to maintain traffic law compliance and adds to overall road safety. Adjust your speed to reflect road conditions, weather, and traffic flow.

8. Watch for pedestrians:

- Keep an eye out for pedestrians, particularly at crosswalks and in high-traffic areas. Pedestrians may emerge unexpectedly, and being alert helps in surrendering the right of way and avoiding accidents.

9. Observe Surrounding Vehicles:

- Pay attention to the conduct of the cars surrounding you. Be mindful of lane changes, turns, and possible problems. Recognizing other drivers' activities enables you to make proactive decisions and changes to your own driving style.

10. Remain Informed About Weather Conditions:

- Be informed of present and expected weather conditions. Rain, snow, fog, and ice all have an affect on visibility and road conditions. To keep your car under control, adjust your driving style and speed appropriately.

11. Mindful Lane Changes

- Exercise care while changing lanes. Check mirrors, utilize turn signals, and do shoulder checks to confirm that the desired lane change is safe and clear of other cars.

12. Be aware of your surroundings:

- Be aware of the general traffic environment. Keep an eye out for merging cars, highway exits and entrances, and be prepared to adjust traffic patterns.

13. Adopt Defensive Driving Techniques:

- Practice defensive driving by predicting other drivers' activities and being ready for unforeseen circumstances. Defensive driving improves your capacity to react to possible threats and increases overall road safety.

3.2 Avoiding Aggressive Driving

3.2.1 Dealing With Road Rage

The word "road rage" refers to aggressive or violent driving conduct. Dealing with road rage is critical to ensuring a safe and peaceful driving environment. Here's a full summary of how to cope with road rage:

1. Remain Calm:

- The first and most important step in dealing with road rage is staying cool. Avoid reacting to violent actions with further aggressiveness. Take deep breaths and concentrate on staying composed.

2. Avoid eye contact:

- If you come across an angry motorist, avoid establishing eye contact. Eye contact might be seen as hostile, perhaps worsening the situation. Keep your focus on the road ahead.

3. Do Not Respond to Aggressive Gestures.

- Ignore hostile gestures or remarks from other drivers. Responding in like might exacerbate the problem. Instead, concentrate on your driving and keep a safe distance.

4. Keep a Safe Distance:

- If an aggressive motorist is tailgating or following you closely, keep a safe distance. Avoid brake checks since quick stops might result in an accident. Allow the aggressive motorist to pass if at all feasible.

5. Do Not Display Aggressive Behavior:

- Do not engage in hostile conduct yourself. Avoid excessive honking, hostile gestures, and retaliation. Responding aggressively merely contributes to the cycle of road rage.

6. Report aggressive behavior:

- If the hostile conduct continues and you feel intimidated, report it to the relevant authorities. Use hands-free alternatives to call law police and share details about the aggressive motorist.

7. Use Safe Driving Practices.

- Prioritize safe driving behaviors, such as respecting traffic regulations, utilizing turn signals, and keeping a steady pace. Predictable and safe driving might help you avoid collisions with aggressive drivers.

8. Create Space

- If an aggressive motorist is tailgating you, make room by switching lanes or pulling over if safe. Allow the aggressive motorist to pass, lowering the chances of a clash.

9. Stay Inside Your Vehicle:

- If challenged by an aggressive motorist, do not get out of your car. Keep windows up and doors secured. If you feel endangered, drive to a public location like a police station.

10. Use a Hands-Free Device.

- If you need to speak with police enforcement or emergency personnel, utilize a hands-free device. Keep your focus on the road and avoid distractions while seeking help.

11. Practice defensive driving:

- Defensive driving is anticipating possible threats and being ready for unforeseen circumstances. Defensive driving may lessen the chance of collisions with aggressive drivers.

12. Maintain perspective:

- Keep in mind that road rage events are often caused by stress, anger, or personal concerns. Do not take hostile actions personally. Concentrate on your personal safety and well-being.

13. Educate yourself:

- Learn about the local regulations governing road rage and aggressive driving. Understanding the legal repercussions of violent action might act as a deterrent.

14. Seek Alternatives:

- If road rage episodes become regular or extreme, try taking other routes, altering your commute time, or utilizing public transit. Prioritize your safety and well-being.

15. Be Patient:

- Patience is essential in preventing road rage incidents. Accept that traffic delays and unexpected incidents are part of the driving experience. Plan ahead of time, leave early, and give yourself additional time to arrive at your location without worry.

Dealing with road rage requires a proactive and calm attitude to safeguard the safety of all drivers. Drivers may help to create a more pleasant and safe driving environment by being cool, practicing defensive driving, and avoiding conflicts. Knowledge of tactics for coping with road rage is essential not just for passing the California DMV Written Test, but also for encouraging responsible and defensive driving.

3.2.2 Remaining Calm in Traffic

Traffic congestion is a regular issue for drivers, and being calm in such circumstances is critical for safe and stress-free driving. Staying cool in traffic reduces the likelihood of road rage incidents, enhances overall road safety, and leads to a more enjoyable driving experience. Here's a comprehensive review of tips for remaining calm in traffic:

1. Plan Ahead:

- Plan your route ahead of time and keep anticipated traffic conditions in mind. Use navigation applications or real-time traffic updates to find the shortest and least crowded routes.

2. Leave early:

- Allow additional time for your travel to accommodate for any unforeseen delays or traffic. Leaving early relieves the need to hurry and allows you to be calm even in traffic.

3. Learn Relaxation Techniques:

- To keep calm, use relaxation methods such as deep breathing and mindfulness. Concentrate on your breath and avoid allowing outside stimuli to influence your emotional state.

4. Listen to Soothing Music or Podcasts.

- Create a relaxing driving atmosphere by listening to music, podcasts, or audiobooks. This might assist to divert you from traffic problems and create a more pleasant environment.

5. Stay Hydrated and Snack Smart.

- Bring a water bottle and some healthy food to remain hydrated and energized. Dehydration and hunger may also cause irritation, so it's important to look after your physical health.

6. Use Comfortable Seating & Temperature:

- To guarantee comfort, adjust your seat and the temperature of the car. Being physically comfortable may improve your mood and help you remain focused while driving.

7. Avoid Distractions:

- Reduce distractions inside the car. Avoid distractions like texting or messing with technological gadgets while driving.

8. Maintain a Positive Mindset.

- Approach traffic delays in a good manner. Use this time to contemplate, listen to instructional stuff, or just relax in isolation. Keeping a pleasant attitude might make the process more tolerable.

9. Practice defensive driving:

- Prepare for traffic situations and practice defensive driving. Prepare for unexpected stops, lane changes, and other drivers' conduct. A proactive strategy might help you manage stress and negotiate traffic more successfully.

10. Accept Factors beyond Your Control:

- Factors outside your control, like as accidents, construction, or weather conditions, often affect traffic flow. Accepting these circumstances and concentrating on what you can control will assist you in remaining calm.

11. Take Breaks as Needed:

- If you notice yourself growing worried or exhausted on your travel, take small pauses. Pull over in a safe area, stretch your legs, and take a few seconds to unwind before continuing.

12. Use Public Transit or Carpooling:

- Look into other modes of transportation, such as public transit or carpooling. Sharing a commute with others may alleviate the stress of driving while also providing opportunity for socialization.

13. Keep a safe following distance:

- Maintain a safe following distance to the car in front of you. This offers a cushion in the event of unexpected stops and minimizes the chance of rear-end crashes, resulting in a more relaxing driving experience.

14. Focus on What You Control:

- Rather of obsessing on problems beyond your control, concentrate on things you can control, such as your driving style, attitude, and responses to traffic situations.

15. Find Joy on the Journey:

- Change your viewpoint and discover delight in the path. Enjoy the landscape, listen to your favorite music, or spend your time thinking pleasant thoughts. A focused approach may turn a stressful journey into a more joyful one.

Staying calm in traffic is a skill that improves overall road safety and personal well-being. By adopting these tactics into your daily driving routine, you may negotiate traffic with a good attitude and decrease the stress that comes with congestion. Knowledge of these approaches is essential not just for passing the California DMV Written Test, but also for fostering safe and stress-free driving behaviors.

CHAPTER 4: VEHICLE OPERATION AND MAINTENANCE

4.1 Vehicle Controls and Instrumentation

4.1.1 Understanding Dashboard Indicators

Dashboard indicators, commonly known as warning lights or symbols, are critical elements of a vehicle's communication system. They offer drivers with critical information on the vehicle's state, warning them to possible problems or requiring action. Understanding these dashboard signs is critical for preserving vehicle health, avoiding problems, and driving safely. Here's a comprehensive list of typical dashboard indicators and their meanings:

1. Check engine light:

- Symbol: It usually resembles an engine.

- Meaning: A check engine light indicates a possible problem with the vehicle's engine or emission control system. It might be a little issue or a big one. To determine the exact issue, a diagnostic scan is recommended.

2. Oil pressure warning light:

- Symbol: An oil container or oil light.

- Meaning: This light indicates low oil pressure. If this light turns on, you must stop immediately since driving with low oil pressure might cause serious engine damage. Check the oil level and, if required, check with a professional.

3. Battery warning light:

- Symbol: Battery symbol.

- The battery warning light indicates a possible problem with the vehicle's charging system. It might indicate a faulty alternator or a dead battery. If this light illuminates, get the charging system examined immediately.

4. Brake system warning light:

- Symbol: Typically, it's an exclamation mark within a circle, occasionally with the word "BRAKE."

- Meaning: This light may signal a variety of concerns, such as low brake fluid, a faulty braking system, or the parking brake being engaged. Brake-related alarms must be addressed quickly for safety reasons.

5. ABS (Anti-lock Brake System) Warning Light:

- Symbol: Typically, the letters ABS are arranged in a circle.

- Meaning: The ABS warning light indicates a problem with the anti-lock brake system. While the vehicle's normal brakes should continue to operate, the ABS system may malfunction, impairing the vehicle's ability to stop under certain situations.

6. Airbag Warning Light:

- Symbol: Typically, this is an airbag icon.

The airbag warning light indicates a problem with the vehicle's airbag system. If this light is on, it may indicate that the airbags will not deploy in the case of a collision. Seek out expert examination and repair.

7. Tire Pressure Monitoring System (TPMS) Light

- Symbol: Typically, it is an exclamation mark within a horseshoe or a tire image with an exclamation mark.

- Meaning: The TPMS light notifies drivers when one or more tires have low tire pressure. Check and adjust tire pressure appropriately. Ignoring this warning might result in poor fuel economy and tire wear.

8. Warning Light for Coolant Temperature

- Symbol: Typically, it's a thermometer symbol or an arrow-shaped wave icon.

- Meaning: This light indicates that the engine is overheated. Stop the car, switch off the engine, and let it cool. Check the coolant level and fix any cooling system problems.

9. Warning Light for Transmission Temperature

- Symbol: It looks like a thermometer inside a gear symbol.

- Meaning: The transmission temperature warning light indicates that the transmission fluid is overheated. Overheating might result in transmission damage. Pull aside, switch off your engine, and let it cool off. Seek expert help if necessary.

10. The Fuel Level Indicator:
- Symbol: A gasoline pump symbol, or simply a gas pump icon.
- Meaning: The fuel level indicator displays the quantity of fuel left in the tank. To prevent running out of petrol, refuel immediately. Some automobiles feature a low-fuel warning light.

11. Reminder about the Seat Belt:
- Symbol: Typically, it's an emblem of a person wearing a seat belt.
- Meaning: The seat belt reminder light instructs the driver and passengers to buckle their seat belts. Before driving, make sure all individuals are securely strapped.

12. High Beam Indicator
- Symbol: Typically, it is a blue symbol that resembles a headlight with lines indicating light beams.
- Meaning: The high beam indication appears when the vehicle's high beams are enabled. It acts as a reminder to switch to low lights while approaching another vehicle.

13. Turn Signal Indicator
- Symbol: Normally, it is an arrow pointing left or right.
- Meaning: When the driver engages the turn signals, the indicator flashes. It is used as a visual indication to notify other drivers of upcoming lane changes or turns.

14. Cruise Control Indicator
- Symbol: Typically, it is a basic symbol of a speedometer or cruise control.
- Meaning: The cruise control indication appears when the cruise control system is activated. It indicates that the car is maintaining a certain speed based on the driver's input.

15. Warning Light for Engine Temperature
- Symbol: Typically, it's a thermometer symbol or an arrow-shaped wave icon.

- Meaning: This light, like the coolant temperature warning light, indicates that the engine is overheating. Immediate care is required to avoid engine damage.

Understanding these dashboard signs is critical for responding quickly and appropriately to any vehicle concerns. Check your vehicle's handbook on a regular basis to get acquainted with various symbols and their meanings. Regular maintenance and early resolution of concerns may assist maintain a safe and dependable driving experience. Knowledge of dashboard indicators is essential for not just passing the California DMV Written Test, but also for responsible car ownership.

4.1.2 adjusting mirrors and seats

The proper adjustment of mirrors and seats in a car is critical for generating an ideal driving experience. Well-adjusted mirrors give a good view of the surrounding traffic, reducing blind spots, while correctly positioned seats improve comfort and control. Here's a full guide on changing the mirrors and seats for the best driving experience:

Adjusting Mirrors

1. Rear View Mirror:

- Position the rearview mirror so that it frames the full back window.

- Make sure the mirror gives a good view of the road behind, reducing the need to turn around while driving.

- Adjust the mirror to prevent glare from headlights at night.

2. Side Mirrors:

- Adjust your side mirrors so that you can see the adjacent lanes without your own car in the mirror (this eliminates blind spots).

- Apply the SAE (Society of Automotive Engineers) method:

- To adjust the driver's side mirror, place your head against the window and adjust it till the side of your car is barely out of vision.

- Lean toward the center of the automobile and adjust the passenger side mirror so the side of your vehicle is barely out of vision.

- Check and adjust mirrors before driving to ensure they are properly aligned.

3. Convex (Blind Spot) Mirrors:

- Some automobiles have convex or blind spot mirrors mounted on the side mirrors.

- Adjust these mirrors to provide a broader field of vision, particularly in blind places.

- Make sure they supplement, rather than duplicate, the information offered by the primary side mirrors.

Adjusting Seats

1. The seat height is:

- Adjust the seat height to guarantee a good view of the dashboard.

- An appropriate height helps the driver to view the road ahead and judge the vehicle's location in relation to other vehicles.

2. Seat position (forward/backward):

- Adjust the seat position so that you can reach the pedals with a modest bend of your knees.

- Leave adequate space between your chest and the steering wheel for airbag deployment in the case of an accident.

3. Seat Recline

- Adjust the seatback to provide a comfortable recline while maintaining support.

- Avoid leaning too far back since it may impair your ability to manage the car and see the road effectively.

4. Steering Wheel Position

- Set the steering wheel height and depth to provide a good view of the instrument cluster.

- The top of the steering wheel should preferably be at or slightly below shoulder height.

5. The Headrest Position:

- Adjust the headrest to match the back of your head, giving support and lowering the risk of whiplash in the event of an accident.

6. Lumbral Support:

- If your car has adjustable lumbar support, use it to give lower back support while maintaining a comfortable driving position.

7. The Armrest Position:

- Adjust the armrests to enable your arms to rest comfortably while maintaining a gentle hold on the driving wheel.

8. Sequence for adjusting the mirrors and seats:

- First, adjust the mirrors to have a good picture of the surroundings.

- Adjust the seat to the proper position using the mirrors' information.

9. Driver Comfort Zone:

- Strive for a mix of comfort and control. A correctly set seat improves control of the vehicle, decreasing tiredness during lengthy rides.

10. Regularly Check and Adjust:

- Check and adjust mirrors and seats on a regular basis to reflect changes in driver preferences or when various people drive the car.

Extra Tips:

- Take test drives:

- Before making any final adjustments, perform brief test drives to check the comfort and efficacy of the mirror and seat placements.

- Think about your own preferences

- Personal preferences may influence adjustment decisions. Experiment with various settings to see what works best for you.

- Putting Safety First:

- Always adjust mirrors and seats when the car is stopped and parked in a safe spot.

- Adapt for Various Drivers:

- If numerous people routinely drive the same car, provide a method for making fast and simple modifications to meet diverse driver preferences.

Properly adjusted mirrors and chairs improve not only the driving enjoyment but also road safety. Regularly evaluating and readjusting these factors ensures that the driving experience is pleasant and favorable to retaining good vehicle control. Knowledge of these modifications is essential for responsible and safe driving habits, and it is a component of the California DMV Written Test.

4.2 Basic vehicle maintenance

4.2.1 Monitoring Fluid Levels

Regularly monitoring your vehicle's fluid levels is an essential part of normal maintenance. Proper fluid levels aid in the smooth functioning and durability of the engine, gearbox, and other critical components. Here's a full guide on checking different fluid levels in your vehicle:

 Engine oil:

1. Park on Level Surfaces:

- To acquire accurate oil level measurements, place the car on a flat surface.

2. Engine Off and Cooling:

- Shut off the engine and let it cool for a few minutes to obtain an accurate oil level measurement.

3. Where to find the oil dipstick:

- Remove the oil dipstick, which is generally a brightly colored handle found near the engine.

4. Wipe and reinsert:

- Wipe the dipstick clean with a towel, completely insert it, then draw it out again to check the oil level.

5. Check the oil level:

- The dipstick contains indications that show the appropriate oil level. Ensure that the oil level is within the permitted range.

6. Oil color and consistency:

- Take note of the color and consistency of the oil. A clean, amber-colored oil is desirable. If the oil looks black or smells burned, it may be time to replace it.

 Transmission Fluid:

1. Refer to the owner's manual.

- Refer to your vehicle's owner's handbook to locate the gearbox dipstick.

2. Engine is running:

- To check the transmission fluid, usually the engine must be running and warm. Follow the manufacturer's directions.

3. Locate and Pull Out the Dipstick:

- Just as when you check your oil, find the transmission dipstick, take it out, and clean it.

4. Check fluid levels:

- Fully reinsert the dipstick and draw it out to check the transmission fluid level. Different cars may have different processes, so consult your owner's handbook.

5. Transmission Fluid Color and Smell

- The transmission fluid should be clear and crimson or pink in hue. A burned odor or a dark tint may signal the need for a fluid replacement.

Brake Fluid:

1. Identify the brake fluid reservoir:

- Find the brake fluid reservoir beneath the hood. It's usually near the brake master cylinder.

2. Check fluid levels:

- The reservoir will be marked with minimum and maximum levels. Keep the brake fluid level within this range.

3. Brake fluid color:

- The brake fluid is often a light golden or amber tint. If it seems black or cloudy, it might be contaminated and needs immediate care.

Coolant:

1. Coolant reservoir:

- Locate the coolant reservoir, which is often a clear plastic tank with minimum and maximum level indicators.

2. Check the coolant level:

- With the engine turned off and cool, check the coolant level to ensure it is within the minimum and maximum marks.

3. Coolant color:

- Coolants are often green, orange, or pink. Discoloration may indicate pollution, necessitating a cooling system flush.

Power Steering Fluid:

1. Find the location of the power steering fluid reservoir:

Identify the power steering fluid reservoir, which is usually located near the power steering pump or along the serpentine belt.

2. Check fluid levels:

- Make that the power steering fluid level is within the acceptable range.

3. Power steering fluid color:

- Most power steering fluid is light brown or crimson. A system flush may be required if the fluid smells dark or burned.

Windshield washer fluid:

1. Check reservoir:

- Locate the windshield washer fluid reservoir, which is usually marked with a blue cap and a windshield symbol.

2. Check fluid levels:

- Check that the windshield washer fluid level is adequate for good viewing.

Extra Tips:

- Follow Manufacturer's Guidelines:

- When checking fluid levels, always follow the manufacturer's directions, since techniques may differ across cars.

- Regular Inspections:

- Check fluid levels on a regular basis, particularly before lengthy travels, to identify any problems early.

- Use the correct fluids:

- Follow the fluid recommendations in your vehicle's owner's handbook.

- Get Professional Help:

- If you are unclear about the fluid levels or observe any irregularities, get expert help to prevent causing harm to your car.

Checking fluid levels is a simple yet crucial element of vehicle maintenance. Regular inspections assist assure the correct operation of critical components and add to your vehicle's overall dependability and safety. This information is essential for not just passing the California DMV Written Test, but also for responsible car ownership and operation.

4.2.2 Tire Maintenance

Proper tire care is critical for vehicle safety, performance, and fuel economy. Regular inspections and upkeep assist to prolong tire life and avoid accidents. Here's a complete guide on maintaining and caring for your vehicle's tires:

1. Check tire pressure:

- frequency:

- Check tire pressure at least once a month, particularly before lengthy excursions.

- Use a Pressure Gauge.

- Take a tire pressure gauge and test the air pressure in each tire, including the spare.

- Please refer to the Owner's Manual:

- The recommended tire pressure may be found in the owner's handbook. This information is often located on a plaque inside the driver's side door jamb or in the glove box.

- Inflate to the recommended pressure.

- If the tire pressure is lower than the acceptable level, inflate them to the appropriate pressure. Overinflation and underinflation may have an impact on tire wear and performance.

2. Inspect tread depth:

- Use a tread depth gauge.

- Use a tread depth gauge to determine the depth of the tire tread. Alternatively, you may do the coin test by placing a penny into the tread with Lincoln's head looking downward. If you can see the top of Lincoln's head, the tread is too low.

- minimum tread depth:

- The minimum permitted tread depth is normally 2/32 inch. For maximum safety, it is recommended that tires be replaced before exceeding this limit.

- Uneven tread wear:

- Uneven tread wear may signal alignment problems or incorrect tire pressure. If identified, seek expert assistance with examination and rectification.

3. Rotation Tires:

- Regular Rotation

- Follow the tire rotation plan specified in the vehicle's owner's handbook. This often occurs every 6,000 to 8,000 miles.

- Promote even wear.

- Regular tire rotation encourages equal wear across all tires, increasing their life and improving overall performance.

4. Balance Tires:

- The Balancing Schedule:

- Balance your tires after they've been rotated or if you experience vibrations while driving.

- Promote Smooth Ride:

- Balancing ensures that the weight is uniformly distributed over the tire, resulting in a smooth and pleasant ride.

5. Alignment Checks

- Regular Alignment Checks

- Schedule frequent tire alignment tests, particularly if you have steering troubles, the car pulls to one side, or the tires wear unevenly.

- Avoid Uneven Wear:

- Proper alignment reduces uneven tire wear, which improves handling and fuel economy.

6. Inspect For Damage:

- Visual Inspection

- Check your tires on a regular basis for cuts, bulges, and other signs of deterioration. Inspect the sidewalls and tread.

- Respond Quickly to Issues:

- Address any obvious damage immediately to avoid future deterioration and assure safety.

7. Check Your Spare Tire:

- Include spare in inspections.

- Include the spare tire in routine checks. Make that it is properly inflated, has appropriate tread, and is in excellent shape.

8. Consider Seasonal Tires

- Winter and summer tires:
- In colder months, consider utilizing winter tires to improve grip on snow and ice. When the weather warms up, switch to summer or all-season tires.

9. Proper Tire Storage:

- OFF-SEASON STORAGE:
- If you are keeping tires for a lengthy period of time, store them in a cool, dry spot away from direct sunlight. Cover your tires if possible.

10. Professional Inspection:

- Periodic Professional Inspection
- Schedule expert inspections at regular intervals to examine tire quality, alignment, and general performance.
- Consult a Professional.
- If you detect any recurring problems or concerns with your tires, see a professional technician for a thorough check.

Extra Tips:

- Rotation Patterns for Tires
- Follow the tire rotation schedule indicated in the vehicle's owner's handbook. Common patterns include front-to-back, crisscross, and others.
- The tire pressure monitoring system (TPMS):
- If your car has a TPMS, pay attention to the warning lights that indicate low tire pressure.

- Avoid Overload:

- Avoid overloading your car, since additional weight may cause greater tire wear and decreased fuel economy.
- The proper lug nut torque is:

- When replacing or rotating tires, tighten the lug nuts to the manufacturer's torque guidelines.

Proper tire maintenance is critical to your vehicle's safety and performance. Regular inspections and adjustments help to improve tire health, fuel economy, and overall driving enjoyment. Knowledge of tire care is essential not just for passing the California DMV Written Test, but also for responsible vehicle ownership and safe driving.

CHAPTER 5: PARKING AND MANEUVERS

5.1 Parking regulations

Understanding and following parking restrictions is critical for preserving traffic order, assuring safety, and minimizing congestion in public areas. Parking restrictions are enforced to ensure that the parking system is fair and structured, catering to the demands of both residents and tourists. Here is a full guide on parking regulations:

On-Street Parking Regulations:

1. Parking Signs

- Read and Understand Signs: Pay special attention to parking signs in the area you want to park. These signs provide important information on parking permits, time limits, and restrictions.

2. Time Limitations:

- Respect Time limitations: Many on-street parking places have time limitations. To prevent penalties or towing, ensure that you are aware of and follow these limitations.

3. Metered Parking:

- Use Parking Meters Properly: Before parking in a metered place, learn how to operate the meter. Pay the needed price and park for the specified period.

4. Parking with a Residential Permit

- Respect Residential Zones: Some places have residential permit parking spaces. Parking in these areas usually needs a valid residential permit. To avoid fines, make sure you follow these requirements.

5. Restrictions on Street Sweeping:

- Be aware of street cleaning schedules: Many cities have set days and hours for street sweeping. Parking restrictions may be in effect during certain times to allow for street work.

Off-street Parking Regulations:

1. Parking lots and garages:

- Follow specified Spaces: Only park in specified parking lots and garages. Avoid taking up several spots or parking in areas designated for certain uses.

2. Parking Spaces That Are Accessible.

- Respect Accessible Spaces: Accessible parking spots are allocated for people with impairments. Only use these parking places if you have a valid disability permit or license plate.

3. Loading Zones:

- Observe Loading Zone Restrictions: Loading zones are intended to facilitate the rapid loading and unloading of products. If you are not actively loading or unloading, do not park in these locations.

4. Fire Lanes:

- Avoid Fire Lanes: Fire lanes are just for emergency vehicles. Parking in fire lanes is unlawful and may hinder emergency personnel.

 General Parking Guidelines:

1. Parallel Parking:

- Practice Parallel Parking Skills: Be familiar with parallel parking, particularly in metropolitan areas where it is frequent. This competence is often examined during driving tests.

2. Distance From Intersections:

- Maintain Distance from Intersections: Comply with local parking restrictions. Parking too near to a junction may reduce visibility and hinder traffic movement.

3. Avoid Double Parking

- Do Not Double Park: Double parking, or parking next to another vehicle that is already parked, is typically not permitted. It impedes traffic and might result in penalties.

4. Observe no parking zones:

- Respect No Parking Areas: No parking zones are created for certain purposes, such as ensuring visibility at junctions or enabling traffic flow. Parking in these zones is prohibited and may result in towing.

5. Meter feed:

- Adhere to Metered Parking Limits: Avoid meter feeding, which is the process of constantly adding money to a parking meter to prolong the time beyond the specified restriction. When the time restriction expires, relocate your car.

6. Abandoned Vehicles

- Report Abandoned Vehicles: If you observe an abandoned car in a parking area, notify local authorities. Abandoned automobiles may add to parking shortages and may be removed.

7. Residential Neighborhoods:

- Respect Residential Parking Restrictions: Certain residential communities have parking restrictions in place to prioritize places for homeowners. To prevent fines, be aware of these requirements.

Enforcement and Penalties

1. parking tickets:

- Pay Attention to Parking Tickets: If you obtain a parking ticket, address it right away. Ignoring citations may result in increased fines and penalties.

2. Towing and impoundment:

- Avoid Towing: Parking in prohibited places such as fire lanes or private property may result in towing. Retrieving a towed car incurs extra charges.

3. boot clamps:

- Prevent Booting: Failure to pay parking penalties may result in the placement of a boot clamp on your vehicle's wheel, limiting further movement until the fines are paid.

Additional considerations:

1. Parking Apps That Use Technology:

- Use Parking applications: Some cities provide smartphone applications that give real-time information about available parking spots, payment alternatives, and limitations. Use these tools to park conveniently.

2. Season Parking Rules:

- Be Aware of Seasonal Changes: Parking laws in certain places may vary seasonally, particularly during the winter months when snow removal is a factor.

3. Community Awareness:

- Remain Informed: Local towns may have their own parking laws and restrictions. Keep up to date on any parking rules that apply to your locality.

4. Permit parking:

- get Permits as Required: In permit-parking locations, get the permits needed to park lawfully. Fines may be imposed for violating permit parking requirements.

Understanding and adhering to parking restrictions is not only necessary for avoiding fines and penalties, but also for fostering efficient traffic flow and guaranteeing the safety and accessibility of public areas. This information is essential for safe and law-abiding driving and is a component of the California DMV Written Test.

5.1.1 Parallel parking

Parallel parking is a basic driving technique in which you place your car parallel to the curb between two other parked automobiles. Mastering this skill is critical for urban driving, where parallel parking is often necessary. Here's a comprehensive tutorial on how to parallel park effectively:

A Step-by-Step Guide to Parallel Parking:

1. Choose an Appropriate Space:

- Look for a parking place that is at least 1.5 times as long as your car. Make sure there is adequate room in front and behind the intended location.

2. Activate the turn signal:

- To parallel park, signal right. Check for approaching traffic and determine whether it is safe to pull over.

3. Position Your Vehicle

- Pull beside the car in front of the open parking spot, leaving approximately 2 feet between yours and theirs. Align the rear bumpers and mirrors.

4. Check Your Surroundings

- Check your mirrors and blind zones for cars, pedestrians, and bicycles. Make sure it is safe to continue with the parking technique.

5. Shift in reverse:

- Put the car into reverse gear.

6. Prepare for Turn:

- Steer quickly to the right. Check your surroundings again before moving forward.

7. Start Backing Up:

- Begin backing up gently, checking both side mirrors and tilting your head to see out the rear window. Continue until your vehicle forms a 45-degree angle with the parked automobile behind you.

8. Straighten the steering wheel:

- When your car has reached a 45-degree angle, move the steering wheel to the left to straighten it. Continue to back up until your car's rear bumper is close to that of the vehicle in front of you.

9. Turn the steering wheel to the right:

- Continue turning the steering wheel to the right to complete the parallel parking procedure. Adjust your location so that your car is equally spaced inside the parking slot.

10. Check the final position:

- Verify your vehicle's location in the parking place. Make any required changes by pulling forwards or backwards.

11. Shift to Drive:

- Once your car is correctly parked, put it in drive and straighten the steering wheel.

12. Final Check

- Check your surroundings again before pulling away from the curb. Ensure that merging back into traffic is safe.

Tips for Parallel Parking:

1. Practice in a controlled environment:

- Before trying parallel parking in more congested regions, practice in an empty parking lot or on a calm street.

2. Reference Points:

- To determine the distance between your car and others, use reference points such as the rearview mirror or rear side windows.

3. Check traffic before exiting:

- Before opening the driver's side door, be sure there is no incoming traffic, bikers, or pedestrians.

4. Use Your Mirrors:

- Use your side mirrors and rearview mirror to determine your closeness to other cars and the curb.

5. Take Your Time.

Parallel parking is a skill that gets better with practice. Take your time, particularly if you're studying or feeling hesitant.

6. Be aware of traffic:

- When parallel parking, keep an eye out for vehicles behind you. If required, yield to enable other cars to pass before proceeding with the move.

7. Consider Your Vehicle's Size:

- For parallel parking, larger cars may need additional space. Take this into mind while choosing a parking space.

8. Be Patient and Calm.

- Remain cool and patient, particularly in congested metropolitan areas. Take a minute to review the parking situation.

9. How to Use Parking Aids:

- Use your vehicle's parking aids, such as rearview cameras or parking sensors, to help with parallel parking.

Parallel parking is an important skill that grows easier with practice. Parallel parking may be learned by adopting a methodical approach and spending time familiarizing yourself with the processes. This ability is not only required to pass the California DMV Driving Test, but it also helps to safe and confident urban driving.

5.1.2 Angle parking

Angle parking, also known as diagonal parking, is a parking arrangement in which automobiles are placed at an angle to the curb or edge of the road. This kind of parking is often found in parking lots, retail malls, and other public areas. Understanding how to correctly perform angle parking is critical for making optimum use of parking places and maintaining the safety of both vehicles and pedestrians. Here is a full guide about angle parking:

Angle Parking:

1. Select a parking space:

- Look for an available angle parking place that is appropriate for the size of your car. Make sure there are no notices forbidding angle parking in the designated location.

2. Activate the turn signal:

- Use your turn signal to indicate you want to angle park. Check for approaching cars and pedestrians.

3. Approach at a Safe Speed

- Approach the parking spot at a safe and steady speed. Be mindful of other cars and people in the area.

4. Align your vehicle:

- Position your car parallel to parked vehicles or the authorized angle parking lines. Make sure your car is centered in the parking place.

5. Check the Surroundings:

- Check your mirrors and blind zones for oncoming cars or pedestrians. Make sure it is safe to continue with the parking technique.

6. Start Turning:

- Begin twisting the steering wheel to enter the parking spot at the proper angle. The angle is usually established by pavement markings or the alignment of neighboring parked cars.

7. Continue steering

- Keep turning until your car is appropriately positioned in the angle parking place. Change your speed and steering as required.

8. Center in the Space:

- Aim to center your car inside the parking place, leaving ample room on both sides for other vehicles and without intruding on neighboring spaces.

9. Shift to park:

- When your car is correctly parked, shift into park (for automatic transmissions) or use the parking brake (for manual transmissions).

10. Check Your Position:

- Check your vehicle's location in the parking area and make any required modifications.

11. Leaving the Space:

- Before exiting an angle parking place, watch for incoming vehicles and pedestrians. Use your turn signal to merge safely into traffic.

Tips for Angle Parking

1. Consider the Designated Angle:

- Remember to park at the correct angle. This is often denoted by painted lines or markers on the road.

2. Be aware of your surroundings.

- When angle parking, you should always be mindful of your surroundings. Look for pedestrians, bicycles, or other cars in the area.

3. Respect Adjacent Spaces.

- Park in a way that respects adjacent parking spots, being sure not to infringe on adjoining cars.

4. Consider Vehicle Size

- When parking at an angle, larger cars may need extra room. Consider the size of your car while selecting parking places.

5. Traffic Flow:

- Park in the direction of traffic flow. Align your car with the traffic flow on the route to guarantee a seamless departure.

6. Use Rear View Cameras:

- If your car has a rearview camera, utilize it to help position your vehicle inside the angle parking spot.

7. Experience in controlled environments:

- Build confidence and enhance your angle parking abilities by practicing in vacant parking spaces or regions with little traffic.

8. Follow Signs and Markings.

- Obey any signs or surface markings that indicate angle parking requirements. Some regions may have special regulations or limits.

Angle parking is a convenient and space-saving method for accommodating many automobiles in parking lots or along roadsides. Angle parking may be executed successfully and securely by following the right process and keeping safety and traffic laws in mind. This ability is useful for both the California DMV Driving Test and daily driving situations.

5.2 Three Point Turns and U-Turns

5.2.1 Making a Three-Point Turn

A three-point turn, often known as a "K-turn" or a "turnabout," is a driving technique that reverses your vehicle's direction in a small area. This strategy is especially beneficial when you're on a tight road or need to change directions on a street with no accessible driveways. Here's a full method for executing a three-point turn:

How to Make a Three-Point Turn:

1. Choose a Suitable Location:

- Look for a broad enough area of road to complete the move safely. Make sure there is no incoming traffic and use your turn signals to express your intention to other cars.

2. Pull Over to the Right.

- Pull over to the right side of the road and stop completely. Check your mirrors for traffic and make sure it's safe to go.

3. Signal and Monitor Traffic:

- Use your left turn signal to announce your intention to cross the road. Look for incoming cars from both directions.

4. Check your blind spots:

- Check over your left shoulder for any cars, bikes, or pedestrians in your blind area.

5. Move to the Left:

- Move to the left side of the road. Move your car across the road until it is near the centerline.

6. Stop and Check Traffic Again.

- Bring your car to a full stop when it is almost across the road. Look for approaching vehicles from all directions, including behind you.

7. Signal and start turning right:

- Use your right turn signal to express your intention to turn right. Turn the steering wheel to the right.

8. Complete the Turn:

- Keep spinning until your car is facing the other way. Make sure your car is correctly positioned on the road.

9. Check Traffic One More Time

- Before continuing, look for approaching traffic in both directions. Make sure it is safe to proceed.

10. Proceed in the New Direction

- Continue in the new route once everything is secure and clear. Accelerate smoothly and blend into traffic.

Tips for executing a three-point turn:

1. Select a Wide Location

- Choose a position with enough width to safely complete the three-point turn without hindering traffic.

2. Be Aware Of Traffic:

- Check for traffic at all times when maneuvering. Make sure there is enough time to safely finish each task.

3. Use turn signals:

- Always use turn signals to indicate your intentions to other drivers.

4. Check your blind spots:

- Before making a turn, look over your shoulder to check for blind spots.

5. Make Smooth Moves:

- Use smooth, controlled steering and accelerating actions to maintain stability and safety throughout the maneuver.

6. Practice in Low-traffic areas:

- If you're new to three-point turns, practice in low-traffic locations until you're comfortable with the move.

7. Follow Local Regulations:

- Be aware of any local rules or traffic signs that may limit your ability to conduct a three-point turn in certain regions.

8. Don't block driveways:

- Make sure you don't block driveways, crossroads, or other access points during the three-point turn.

Making a three-point turn is a useful ability for traversing small roadways and changing directions when other choices are unavailable. Practice and familiarity with the processes required can increase your confidence in completing this move, whether on the California DMV Driving Test or in real-world driving situations.

5.2.2 Executing Safe U-Turns

A U-turn is a driving move that requires turning 180 degrees to reverse the direction of travel. To make a safe U-turn, you must pay close attention, use your signals, and follow traffic rules. Here's a complete tutorial on safe U-turns:

Identifying Appropriate Locations:

1. Look for U-Turn signs:

- Look for traffic signs that state whether U-turns are permitted or forbidden. Obey posted signs and respect local restrictions.

2. Choose A Safe and Legal Location:

- Select a place where U-turns are legal and safe to make. Avoid doing U-turns in places with excessive signs or traffic.

Performing the U-Turn:

1. Signal Your Intent:

- Use your turn signal to indicate you want to perform a U-turn. This warns other drivers and contributes to a safe environment.

2. Check the Traffic:

- Look for incoming vehicles from both directions. Make sure you have a clear and enough spacing to safely perform the U-turn.

3. Check for Pedestrians:

- Watch for people crossing the road. Yield to pedestrians at crosswalks and make sure they have cleared the road before making the U-turn.

4. Position Your Vehicle

- Move your car to the far left side of the road, or into a left-turn lane if possible. Make sure you are securely positioned on the road.

5. Check your rearview and side mirrors:

- Check your rearview and side mirrors for oncoming vehicles. Take note of the cars' speeds and distances.

6. Wait for a safe gap.

- Watch for a safe space in incoming traffic. Make sure there is adequate time to perform the U-turn without generating disturbances or confrontations.

7. Complete the U-turn:

- When a safe space is available, move the steering wheel to the left and do the U-turn. To prevent unexpected movements, be sure to turn smoothly and controlled.

8. Check for Cross Traffic

- As you do the U-turn, keep an eye out for vehicles coming from side streets or driveways. Make sure you are not blocking the way of other cars.

9. Stay in the Correct Lane.

- After doing the U-turn, be sure you're in the right lane and aligned with the flow of traffic in the new direction.

10. Activate the right turn signal:

- If required, engage your right turn signal to indicate that you are exiting the U-turn and merging into traffic.

Tips for Safe U-Turns:

1. Use Designated U-Turn Areas.

- Whenever feasible, utilize designated U-turn zones or junctions with U-turn lanes. These areas are intended for safer movement.

2. Be patient.

- Wait patiently for a safe traffic gap. Avoid doing fast or abrupt U-turns, particularly at crowded junctions.

3. Visibility Is Important:

- Before trying a U-turn, be sure you have sufficient vision. Avoid doing U-turns on curves or slopes with restricted sight.

4. Check Local Traffic Laws:

- Be informed with your local traffic rules involving U-turns. Some places may have particular rules regarding U-turns.

5. Avoiding U-Turns Near Intersections:

- Avoid doing U-turns at or near junctions, since this may interrupt traffic flow and increase the danger of crashes.

6. Consider Alternative Routes:

- If performing a U turn seems difficult or dangerous, consider taking another route that allows for a safer change of direction.

7. Practice in Low-traffic areas:

- If you're new to doing U-turns, start in low-traffic areas to gain confidence and familiarity with the procedure.

Drivers must be able to make safe U-turns in order to navigate efficiently and change their routes. Following these principles and paying attention to traffic circumstances will allow you to perform U-turns safely and responsibly, contributing to overall road safety.

CHAPTER 6: SPECIAL LICENSE CONSIDERATIONS

6.1 Commercial Drivers License (CDL) Requirements

6.1.1 CDL Classes & Endorsements

Individuals who drive big, heavy, or specialized vehicles for business reasons must possess a business Driver's License (CDL). CDL courses and endorsements are important components of the licensing system since they describe the sorts of vehicles that a driver is qualified to operate and indicate any extra skills or knowledge they have. Here is a complete guide to CDL courses and endorsements:

CDL classes:

CDL classes divide commercial vehicles depending on their weight, design, and function. There are three primary CDL classes:

1. Class A:

- Vehicles Covered: This class comprises combination vehicles whose total weight exceeds 10,000 pounds when towed.

- Examples include tractor-trailers, truck-and-trailer combos, livestock carriers, and flatbeds.

2. Class B:

- Vehicles Covered: Class B CDL applies to single vehicles with a gross vehicle weight rating (GVWR) of 26,001 pounds or more, as well as vehicles pulling trailers weighing 10,000 pounds or less.

- Examples include large buses, box trucks, dump vehicles, and delivery trucks.

3. Class C:

- Vehicles Covered: Class C CDL is for vehicles capable of transporting 16 or more people (including the driver) or hazardous items in amounts that need placards.

- Examples include small buses, passenger vans, and hazardous transport trucks.

CDL Endorsements:

CDL endorsements are supplementary credentials or certificates that enable a driver to operate certain vehicles or carry specified kinds of goods. Here are some typical CDL endorsements:

1. H (hazardous Materials):

- Requirements: Drivers must pass a written exam and have their backgrounds checked before transporting hazardous items.

- Examples include chemicals, gasses, and flammable or explosive materials.

2. N (Tank Vehicle):

- Requirements: Drivers of vehicles intended to carry liquids or gasses in bulk must meet these requirements.

- Examples are tanker trucks.

3. P (passenger):

- Requirements: Required for drivers of vehicles capable of transporting 16 or more passengers.

- Examples include buses, shuttles, and big passenger vehicles.

4. S (school bus):

- Requirements: For drivers who operate school buses. Typically, extra training and testing are necessary.

- Examples include school buses.

5. T (Double/Triple Trailers):

- Requirements: Double or triple trailer drivers must meet these requirements.

- Examples include long combination vehicles.

6. X (Combination of Tank and Hazardous Material):

- Requirements: This endorsement is required for drivers that carry hazardous items, as well as liquids or gasses in bulk.

7. W(towed trailer):

- Requirements: Tow truck drivers who tow cars weighing 10,000 pounds or more must meet the following requirements.

8. P (passenger transportation):

- Requirements: For drivers of vehicles that can carry 16 or more people (including the driver) but are not for hire.

Obtaining CDL Classes and Endorsements:

1. CDL classes:

- To earn a CDL, applicants must normally pass written knowledge examinations for the particular class they are seeking, complete a skills test, and fulfill additional state-specific criteria.

2. CDL Endorsement:

- Endorsements are gained by passing supplementary written examinations tailored to the kind of vehicle or cargo that the driver desires to convey. Background checks are also required for hazardous materials endorsements.

Renewing and maintaining CDL Classes and Endorsements:

1. Renewal:

- CDL holders are required to renew their licenses on a regular basis, which may entail retesting and completing certain endorsement criteria.

2. Continuous Education:

- Some endorsements, particularly those for hazardous goods or school buses, may need ongoing training and recertification.

3. Medical examinations:

- CDL holders must often undergo medical exams to ensure they are physically fit for the responsibilities of commercial driving.

Understanding the CDL class and endorsement procedures is critical for prospective commercial drivers. It guarantees that drivers are appropriately qualified to operate certain kinds of vehicles and transport varied cargoes, hence contributing to overall road safety. Because restrictions differ per state, people should verify with their state's

Department of Motor Vehicles or other applicable authorities for precise requirements and procedures.

6.1.2 CDL Testing Procedures

Obtaining a Commercial Driver's License (CDL) entails a series of examinations designed to evaluate a candidate's knowledge, abilities, and competence to drive commercial vehicles safely. The CDL testing methods are intended to verify that drivers satisfy the requirements for various CDL classes and endorsements. Here is a thorough guide on CDL testing procedures:

1. Knowledge Tests:

1. General Knowledge Test:

- All CDL candidates must complete a general knowledge exam covering the fundamentals of commercial driving, such as traffic regulations, vehicle inspection, and safe driving practices.

2. Endorsement knowledge tests:

- Applicants seeking specialized endorsements, such as Hazardous Materials (H), Tank Vehicles (N), or Passenger (P), must complete extra knowledge examinations unique to the endorsement they are seeking.

3. Air Brake Test

- Required for drivers of cars equipped with air brakes. It discusses the concepts of air brake operation, inspection, and maintenance.

2. Skills Tests:

1. Pre-trip inspection:

- Candidates are assessed on their competence to check a commercial vehicle to verify it is safe to operate. This involves inspecting different components such as brakes, lights, tires, and coupling mechanisms.

2. The Basic Control Skills Test:

- This exam measures a driver's ability to operate a commercial vehicle in a variety of movements, including straight-line backing, offset backing, and parallel parking.

3. On-Road Driving Test

- The on-road driving exam assesses a candidate's competence to drive a commercial vehicle safely in a variety of traffic circumstances. It encompasses merging, lane changes, turns, and general vehicle control.

3. Endorsement-Specific Testing:

1. Endorsement: Hazardous Materials (H)

- In addition to the written exam, applicants seeking the Hazardous Materials endorsement must take a security threat assessment. This endorsement is subject to federal restrictions, and background checks are done.

2. Endorsement for Tank Vehicles (N)

- The Tank Vehicles endorsement exam assesses a driver's knowledge and abilities in the safe operation of vehicles that carry liquids or gasses in bulk.

3. Endorsement by a Passenger (P)

- Candidates for the Passenger endorsement must show their competence to properly drive vehicles capable of transporting 16 or more people. This covers the correct loading and unloading methods.

4. Endorsement for School Bus (S)

- Obtaining the School Bus endorsement often requires extra examination on areas such as kid loading and unloading, emergency procedures, and school bus operator rules.

4. Additional considerations:

1. State-specific requirements:

- CDL testing methods differ by state, therefore applicants should acquaint themselves with their state's particular standards and procedures.

2. Medical Exam:

- CDL candidates must have a medical exam done by a qualified medical examiner. The test evaluates the driver's physical and mental fitness for commercial driving.

3. Written test scores:

- Candidates must pass the written examinations before they may take the skills tests.

5. CDL training programs:

1. CDL training schools:

- Many applicants choose to participate in CDL training programs provided by approved colleges. These programs include classroom education, hands-on training, and help with written and skills assessments.

2. Practice Tests

- Practice exams are accessible online or via training programs to assist applicants get comfortable with the structure and content of written examinations.

6. Renewal and Endorsement Maintenance:

1. Renewal:

- CDL holders are required to renew their licenses on a regular basis, which may entail retesting and completing certain endorsement criteria.

2. Continuous Education:

- Periodic training and recertification may be required for certain endorsements to ensure that drivers are up to date on current rules and safety practices.

Understanding CDL testing protocols is critical for anybody interested in becoming a commercial driver. It guarantees that drivers have received proper training, testing, and qualifications to operate commercial vehicles safely and responsibly on the road. Because restrictions differ by state, applicants should check with their state's Department of Motor Vehicles or other applicable body for particular requirements and processes.

6.2 Motorcycle License

6.2.1 Motorcycle License Requirements

Obtaining a motorcycle license requires passing particular standards to guarantee that riders have the knowledge and abilities needed to drive a motorbike safely. Motorcycle license requirements vary by state, but they usually consist of a mix of written examinations, skills tests, and, in some circumstances, completion of a motorcycle safety course. Here's a complete guide on motorbike licensing requirements.

1. Minimum age requirement:

1. Varies by state:

The minimum age for obtaining a motorbike license varies by state. In many states, you must be at least 16 or 18 years old to apply for a motorbike license.

2. Learner's Permit

1. Written examination:

- To get a learner's permit, most states require prospective motorcyclists to complete a written examination. This test usually includes motorcycle-specific regulations, traffic legislation, and safe riding techniques.

2. Vision Test:

- A vision test is often necessary to guarantee that motorcyclists have enough eyesight to ride a motorbike safely.

3. Restrictions on the Learner's Permit

- Once awarded a learner's permit, cyclists may face limitations like as not riding at night, not carrying passengers, or always being accompanied by a licensed rider.

3. Motorcycle safety course:

1. Optional, but recommended:

- Many states provide optional motorcycle safety courses that combine classroom teaching with hands-on riding experience. Riders who complete such a course may be excluded from completing the skills exam and, in certain situations, get insurance reductions.

4. Skills Test:

1. On-Road Skills Testing:

- Riders are often required to complete an on-road skills test to show their ability to ride a motorbike safely. This exam may entail turning, stopping, and maneuvering between cones.

2. Motorcycle Inspection:

- Some jurisdictions may require applicants to do a basic motorcycle examination to demonstrate they understand the vehicle's components and safety features.

5. Written exam for full license.

1. Written Exam For Motorcycles:

- To earn a complete motorbike license, motorcyclists must usually pass a motorcycle-specific written test. This test includes subjects such as motorcycle operation, traffic laws, and safety precautions.

6. Additional requirements for minors:

1. Parental consent:

- In certain jurisdictions, those under a specific age (often 18) may need parental permission to get a motorbike license.

2. Driver's License Prerequisites:

- In certain states, persons must hold a valid driver's license before acquiring a motorbike license.

7. Motorcycle License Renewal:

1. Renewal Period

- Motorcycle licenses, like driver's licenses, have a renewal term. Riders must renew their licenses at the prescribed interval, which is normally every few years.

8. Endorsement on the driver's license:

1. Adding a motorcycle endorsement:

- Instead of acquiring a separate motorcycle license, several jurisdictions allow motorcyclists to add a motorbike endorsement to their current driver's license. This includes passing the relevant written and skills tests.

9. Proof of insurance:

1. Insurance Requirements:

- Some states may require riders to present evidence of motorcycle insurance in order to acquire or renew their license.

10. Understanding the Local Regulations:

1. State-Specific Variation:

- The qualifications for a motorcycle license might vary greatly across states. Individuals must get acquainted with their state's particular rules and practices.

11. Continuing education:

1. Advanced Training Courses:

- Riders are urged to take advanced motorcycle training courses to improve their abilities and increase their safety knowledge. Some states give advanced courses that may result in perks like license point reductions or insurance savings.

Individuals who want to ride motorbikes lawfully must first understand and meet motorcycle licensing criteria. Checking with your local Department of Motor Vehicles or appropriate licensing body is critical for staying up to speed on individual state rules, protocols, and any current revisions to motorcycle licensing procedures.

6.2.2 Safer Riding Practices

Motorcycle riders must acquire and continuously exercise safe riding habits in order to lower the chance of accidents and improve overall road safety. Safe riding methods include a mix of expertise, awareness, and responsible conduct. Here's a full guide on important safe riding behaviors for motorcyclists:

1. Protective Gear:

1. Helmet:

- Always wear a well-fitting helmet that satisfies safety regulations. Helmets offer essential head protection in the case of an accident.

2. Protective clothing:

- Wear robust and protective clothes such as coats, trousers, gloves, and boots to reduce the chance of harm in the event of a fall or accident.

3. Visibility Gear

- Select gear with high-visibility characteristics to increase your visibility to other drivers.

2. Pre-ride inspection:

1. Check Your Tires

- Check your tire pressure and tread depth on a regular basis. Properly inflated tires provide superior handling and traction.

2. Fluid Levels

- To keep the motorbike in good operating order, check the brake fluid, oil, and coolant levels on a regular basis.

3. Lights and Signals:

- Before each ride, check that all lights and signals are working correctly.

3. Riding skills:

1. Training Classes:

- Enroll in a motorcycle safety instruction class to improve your riding abilities. Many courses include both classroom teaching and hands-on riding experience.

2. Practice Emergency Maneuvers

- Practice emergency maneuvers on a regular basis, including rapid stops and evasive maneuvers, to improve your abilities in crucial circumstances.

3. Understanding Motorcycle Dynamics:

- Learn how a motorbike reacts in various situations, such as rainy or slick roads. Adapt your riding style appropriately.

4. Defensive Riding:

1. Constant Awareness:

- Maintain constant vigilance and awareness of your surroundings. Scan the road ahead, check your mirrors constantly, and anticipate possible risks.

2. Keep a safe following distance:

- Maintain a safe distance from the car in front of you to allow you sufficient response time in the event of an abrupt stop or emergency.

3. Be Visible:

- Make yourself visible to other drivers by utilizing headlights, wearing brightly colored clothing, and placing yourself properly inside your lane.

5. Weather Considerations:

1. Adjust Riding for the Weather

- Adjust your riding style in inclement weather situations. On wet or slick roads, drive slowly, increase following distances, and use care.

2. Visibility in Poor Conditions

- Use reflective clothing and turn signals to improve visibility, particularly in low light or in bad weather.

6. Riding within the limits:

1. Understanding Your Limitations:

- Ride within your ability level and avoid taking excessive risks. As your experience grows, you may graduate to more difficult rides.

2. How to Avoid Riding Fatigue:

- Fatigue impairs judgment and response time. Take stops when riding long distances to keep awake and focused.

7. Intersections and Traffic:

1. Scan for traffic:

- Thoroughly monitor junctions for approaching traffic and be prepared for rapid maneuvers by other cars.

2. Right-of-way awareness:

- Understand and observe right-of-way regulations, and never assume other cars will notice you.

8. Riding Groups:

1. Communication:

- Use unambiguous communication signals with other riders to indicate turns, stops, and dangers.

2. Keep Formation:

- Ride in a staggered configuration to maximize visibility and give each rider more room.

9. Post-ride maintenance:

1. Check for Damage:

- After each ride, evaluate your motorbike for indicators of damage or difficulties that need care.

2. Regular Service:

- Follow the manufacturer's suggested service schedule to keep the motorbike in peak condition.

10. Legal and Ethical Riding:

1. Follow Traffic Laws:

- Follow speed limits, traffic lights, and all other traffic rules. Respect your fellow road users.

2. Do not drink and ride:

- Never ride while under the influence of alcohol or drugs. Impaired driving considerably raises the likelihood of an accident.

11. Continuous Learning:

1. Stay Informed:

- Keep up with current safety recommendations, riding styles, and road restrictions. Continuous learning helps you become a more proficient and safe rider.

Both rookie and expert motorcyclists must follow safe riding habits. By continuously applying these measures, motorcyclists contribute to their own and others' road safety. Regularly updating skills via extra training and being up to date on the newest safety advice improves a rider's ability to traverse the roadways safely.

Practice Tests

Instructions:

Read each question carefully.

Choose the best answer for each question.

At the end of the test, check your answers against the provided explanations.

If you are unsure about an answer, make your best guess.

Practice Test 1: Rules of the Road

Questions

1. What does a yellow traffic sign with a curved arrow indicate?

a. Caution - Slippery Road Ahead

b. Right Turn Only

c. Winding Road Ahead

d. No Passing Zone

2. What is the purpose of a solid yellow line on the roadway?

a. Indicates the center of the road

b. Marks the edge of the road

c. Separates lanes of traffic moving in opposite directions

d. Allows passing if safe to do so

3. When are you allowed to pass another vehicle on the right?

a. When the vehicle ahead is making a left turn

b. Only in residential areas

c. On one-way streets

d. When there is a broken yellow line on your side

4. What should you do when you approach a school bus with flashing red lights and a stop sign extended?

a. Pass the bus with caution

b. Slow down and proceed with caution

c. Stop and remain stopped until the lights stop flashing and the stop sign is retracted

d. Honk your horn to alert the bus driver

5. What does a white rectangular sign with black lettering indicate?

a. School Crossing

b. Warning - Construction Zone

c. Stop Sign Ahead

d. Pedestrian Crossing

14. When can you make a U-turn at an intersection with a traffic light?

a. Always, if there is no oncoming traffic

b. Only when the light is green

c. Only when the light is red

d. When the intersection is clear of other vehicles

15. What should you do when you see a pedestrian with a white cane or guide dog at a crosswalk?

a. Proceed with caution

b. Honk your horn to alert them

c. Yield the right-of-way

d. Accelerate to clear the crosswalk quickly

16. What does a blue circular sign with a white arrow indicate?

a. Mandatory Roundabout Ahead

b. One-Way Traffic

c. Keep Right

d. Detour Ahead

17. When approaching a railroad crossing with flashing lights and gates, what should you do?

a. Proceed with caution

b. Stop and wait until the lights stop flashing and the gates are fully raised

c. Drive around the gates if no train is visible

d. Speed up to clear the tracks quickly

18. What does a double yellow line on the roadway indicate?

a. No passing in either direction

b. Passing is allowed in both directions

c. Passing is allowed only on the left

d. Passing is allowed only on the right

19. What does a red and white triangular sign with an exclamation mark indicate?

a. Caution - Slippery When Wet

b. Warning - Steep Grade Ahead

c. Stop Ahead

d. Yield Ahead

20. What is the purpose of rumble strips on the roadway?

a. To alert drivers to slow down

b. To indicate the edge of the road

c. To create a smooth driving surface

d. To enhance traction in icy conditions

Answers

11. b. Stop

12. c. When changing lanes or turning

13. b. Warning - Construction Zone

14. d. When the intersection is clear of other vehicles

15. c. Yield the right-of-way

16. c. Keep Right

17. b. Stop and wait until the lights stop flashing and the gates are fully raised

18. a. No passing in either direction

19. b. Warning - Steep Grade Ahead

20. a. To alert drivers to slow down

Explanation

11. A red octagonal sign with white lettering indicates a stop sign.

12. Turn signals should be used when changing lanes or turning.

13. A yellow diamond-shaped sign with black symbols usually indicates a warning for a construction zone.

14. U-turns at intersections with traffic lights are allowed when the intersection is clear of other vehicles.

15. When encountering a pedestrian with a white cane or guide dog at a crosswalk, you must yield the right-of-way.

16. A blue circular sign with a white arrow typically indicates "Keep Right."

17. When approaching a railroad crossing with flashing lights and gates, you must stop and wait until the lights stop flashing and the gates are fully raised.

18. A double yellow line on the roadway indicates no passing in either direction.

19. A red and white triangular sign with an exclamation mark indicates a warning for a steep grade ahead.

20. Rumble strips on the roadway are designed to alert drivers to slow down or veer off the road.

21. What is the meaning of a red traffic sign with a white downward-pointing arrow?

a. Yield the right-of-way

b. No Right Turn

c. One-Way Traffic Only

d. Stop Ahead

22. When must you dim your headlights when approaching an oncoming vehicle at night?

a. Only in residential areas

b. Within 500 feet of the oncoming vehicle

c. Within 1,000 feet of the oncoming vehicle

d. When the oncoming vehicle signals you to dim your lights

23. What does a solid white line on the roadway indicate?

a. Marks the edge of the road

b. Separates lanes of traffic moving in opposite directions

c. Allows passing if safe to do so

d. Indicates the center of the road

24. What should you do when you encounter a yellow flashing traffic signal?

a. Come to a complete stop

b. Proceed with caution

c. Accelerate to clear the intersection quickly

d. Make a U-turn

25. What does a pentagon-shaped sign with a yellow background indicate?

a. School Zone Ahead

b. Stop Sign Ahead

c. No Passing Zone

d. Warning - School Crossing

26. How should you position your hands on the steering wheel when driving?

a. Any comfortable position

b. 10 and 2 o'clock positions

c. 9 and 3 o'clock positions

d. 8 and 4 o'clock positions

27. What is the primary purpose of a crossbuck sign at a railroad crossing?

a. To indicate the speed limit

b. To warn of an upcoming intersection

c. To mark the location of a railroad crossing

d. To indicate a pedestrian crossing

28. What does a yellow and black circular sign with an X-shaped symbol indicate?

a. Railroad Crossing Ahead

b. Do Not Enter

c. Hazardous Materials Zone

d. Stop Ahead

29. When should you use your high-beam headlights?

a. When driving in foggy conditions

b. When following another vehicle closely

c. When driving in well-lit urban areas

d. When approaching oncoming traffic

30. What is the purpose of a regulatory sign?

a. Provides information about points of interest

b. Indicates speed limits and traffic regulations

c. Warns of potential hazards

d. Provides directions to specific locations

Answers

21. c. One-Way Traffic Only

22. b. Within 500 feet of the oncoming vehicle

23. d. Indicates the center of the road

24. b. Proceed with caution

25. a. School Zone Ahead

26. c. 9 and 3 o'clock positions

27. c. To mark the location of a railroad crossing

28. a. Railroad Crossing Ahead

29. a. When driving in foggy conditions

30. b. Indicates speed limits and traffic regulations

Explanation

21. A red traffic sign with a white downward-pointing arrow indicates one-way traffic only.

22. Dim your headlights when approaching an oncoming vehicle within 500 feet.

23. A solid white line on the roadway indicates the center of the road.

24. When encountering a yellow flashing traffic signal, proceed with caution.

25. A pentagon-shaped sign with a yellow background typically indicates a school zone ahead.

26. The recommended hand positions on the steering wheel are 9 and 3 o'clock.

27. The primary purpose of a crossbuck sign at a railroad crossing is to mark the location of the crossing.

28. A yellow and black circular sign with an X-shaped symbol usually indicates a railroad crossing ahead.

29. Use high-beam headlights when driving in foggy conditions to improve visibility.

30. Regulatory signs indicate speed limits and traffic regulations, guiding drivers on rules they must follow.

31. What is the correct procedure when approaching a stop sign at an intersection?

a. Slow down, and proceed through the intersection without stopping

b. Come to a complete stop, and proceed when it's safe to do so

c. Honk your horn and proceed without stopping

d. Yield the right-of-way to vehicles on the left

32. What does a white rectangular sign with black lettering and a red circle indicate?

a. Stop Sign Ahead

b. No Parking Zone

c. Speed Limit

d. Yield Right of Way

33. When are you allowed to use your vehicle's horn?

a. To alert other drivers of your presence

b. To express frustration or annoyance

c. To signal your approval of another driver's actions

d. Only in emergencies to avoid a collision

34. What does a green arrow traffic signal indicate?

a. Proceed with caution

b. Stop

c. Yield the right-of-way

d. Turn in the direction of the arrow when safe

35. What should you do when you approach a traffic signal displaying a steady yellow light?

a. Speed up to clear the intersection quickly

b. Stop if it is safe to do so

c. Proceed with caution

d. Make a U-turn

36. What is the purpose of a red and white triangular sign with a red border?

a. Stop Sign Ahead

b. Warning - Yield Ahead

c. No Passing Zone

d. Warning - Stop Ahead

37. When can you proceed through an intersection after a stop at a stop sign?

a. After checking for oncoming traffic and pedestrians

b. Only when other vehicles honk at you

c. As soon as you come to a complete stop

d. After yielding the right-of-way to vehicles on the left

38. What does a black and yellow circular sign with a picture of a deer indicate?

a. Warning - School Zone

b. Deer Crossing

c. Hazardous Materials Zone

d. Stop Ahead

39. When are you allowed to pass a school bus with flashing red lights and a stop sign extended?

a. When the bus is on the opposite side of a divided highway

b. Never, unless directed by a police officer

c. When the bus is on a residential street

d. Only if you are in a hurry

40. What does a double white line on the roadway indicate?

a. No passing in either direction

b. Passing is allowed in both directions

c. Passing is allowed only on the left

d. Passing is allowed only on the right

Answers

31. b. Come to a complete stop, and proceed when it's safe to do so

    32. a. Stop Sign Ahead

    33. a. To alert other drivers of your presence

    34. d. Turn in the direction of the arrow when safe

    35. c. Proceed with caution

    36. d. Warning - Stop Ahead

37. a. After checking for oncoming traffic and pedestrians

38. b. Deer Crossing

39. a. When the bus is on the opposite side of a divided highway

40. a. No passing in either direction

Explanation

31. When approaching a stop sign, come to a complete stop and proceed when it's safe to do so.

32. A white rectangular sign with black lettering and a red circle indicates an upcoming stop sign.

33. Use your vehicle's horn to alert other drivers of your presence, not to express frustration.

34. A green arrow traffic signal allows you to turn in the direction of the arrow when safe.

35. When approaching a steady yellow light, proceed with caution, as the signal is about to turn red.

36. A red and white triangular sign with a red border indicates a warning for an upcoming stop sign.

37. After stopping at a stop sign, proceed through the intersection only after checking for oncoming traffic and pedestrians.

38. A black and yellow circular sign with a picture of a deer indicates a deer crossing warning.

39. Passing a school bus with flashing red lights and a stop sign extended is allowed when the bus is on the opposite side of a divided highway.

40. A double white line on the roadway indicates no passing in either direction.

41. What does a red and white triangular sign with a red border and the word "AHEAD" indicate?

a. Warning - Yield Ahead

b. Warning - Stop Ahead

c. School Zone Ahead

d. Construction Zone Ahead

42. What does a circular green traffic sign with the word "EXIT" indicate?

a. Warning - Exit Ahead

b. No Exit

c. Exit Ramp Ahead

d. Yield the Right-of-Way

43. When is it legal to use a handheld mobile phone while driving?

a. Only when at a red traffic signal

b. When using the speakerphone function

c. When driving in rural areas with low traffic

d. Never, unless in case of emergency

44. What should you do when approaching a yield sign?

a. Speed up to merge quickly with traffic

b. Come to a complete stop, and yield the right-of-way to other traffic

c. Merge into traffic without slowing down

d. Ignore the sign and proceed at your normal speed

45. What is the purpose of a white diamond-shaped sign with black symbols?

a. No Passing Zone

b. Warning - School Zone

c. Construction Zone Ahead

d. Pedestrian Crossing

46. What does a black and white circular sign with a red slash and the word "NO" indicate?

a. No Parking Zone

b. No U-turn

c. No Left Turn

d. No Right Turn

47. When should you use your vehicle's hazard lights?

a. When double-parked in a busy street

b. During inclement weather or low visibility

c. When approaching a green traffic light

d. Only when parked on the shoulder of a highway

48. What does a yellow and black diamond-shaped sign with the word "LANE" indicate?

a. Merge Left

b. Right Turn Only

c. Left Turn Only

d. Lane Ends

49. What does a white rectangular sign with black symbols indicate?

a. Stop Sign Ahead

b. Speed Limit

c. No Parking Zone

d. Yield the Right-of-Way

50. When is it legal to pass another vehicle on the right?

a. When the vehicle is making a left turn

b. Only in designated passing zones

c. When the vehicle is slowing down for a yellow light

d. Never, unless driving on a one-way street

Answers

41. b. Warning - Stop Ahead

    42. c. Exit Ramp Ahead

    43. d. Never, unless in case of emergency

    44. b. Come to a complete stop, and yield the right-of-way to other traffic

    45. a. No Passing Zone

    46. b. No U-turn

    47. b. During inclement weather or low visibility

    48. a. Merge Left

    49. c. No Parking Zone

    50. d. Never, unless driving on a one-way street

Explanation

    41. A red and white triangular sign with a red border and the word "AHEAD" indicates a warning for an upcoming stop sign.

    42. A circular green traffic sign with the word "EXIT" indicates an upcoming exit ramp.

    43. Using a handheld mobile phone while driving is illegal in most places, except in emergencies.

    44. When approaching a yield sign, come to a complete stop and yield the right-of-way to other traffic.

    45. A white diamond-shaped sign with black symbols indicates a no passing zone.

    46. A black and white circular sign with a red slash and the word "NO" indicates a prohibition, such as no U-turn.

    47. Hazard lights should be used during inclement weather or low visibility to alert other drivers.

    48. A yellow and black diamond-shaped sign with the word "LANE" indicates that a specific lane is ending.

    49. A white rectangular sign with black symbols typically provides information about specific regulations or conditions.

    50. Passing another vehicle on the right is generally allowed only when driving on a one-way street.

51. What does a yellow and black circular sign with a picture of a truck indicate?

a. Truck Route

b. No Trucks Allowed

c. Truck Weigh Station Ahead

d. Warning - Trucks Turning

52. When is it appropriate to use your vehicle's high-beam headlights?

a. In well-lit urban areas

b. When following another vehicle closely

c. On poorly lit roads and in rural areas without oncoming traffic

d. Only during adverse weather conditions

53. What should you do when you see a "DO NOT ENTER" sign?

a. Make a U-turn and proceed in the opposite direction

b. Stop and wait for permission to enter

c. Continue straight ahead

d. Merge into traffic without slowing down

54. What does a red and white triangular sign with the word "YIELD" indicate?

a. Stop Sign Ahead

b. Merge Ahead

c. Right-of-Way Ahead

d. Yield the Right-of-Way

55. What does a green rectangular sign with white lettering indicate?

a. No Parking Zone

b. Guide Sign

c. Regulatory Sign

d. Informational Sign

56. When should you use your vehicle's parking lights?

a. Only during nighttime

b. When parked on a busy street

c. In place of headlights during inclement weather

d. Only when driving in residential areas

57. What does a black and yellow circular sign with a picture of a bicycle indicate?

a. Bicycle Lane

b. Warning - Bicycles Crossing

c. No Bicycles Allowed

d. Bicycle Parking

58. What is the purpose of a white rectangular sign with black lettering and a red circle with a line through it?

a. No Parking Zone

b. No Left Turn

c. Do Not Enter

d. No U-turn

59. When are you allowed to pass a vehicle stopped at a crosswalk for pedestrians?

a. Only if pedestrians are not present

b. When the vehicle is a commercial truck

c. Never, unless directed by a police officer

d. Only if pedestrians have already crossed

60. What does a blue rectangular sign with white lettering indicate?

a. Hospital Zone Ahead

b. Informational Sign

c. Rest Area Ahead

d. Service Area Ahead

Answers

51. a. Truck Route

    52. c. On poorly lit roads and in rural areas without oncoming traffic

    53. a. Make a U-turn and proceed in the opposite direction

    54. d. Yield the Right-of-Way

    55. b. Guide Sign

    56. a. Only during nighttime

    57. a. Bicycle Lane

    58. c. Do Not Enter

    59. c. Never, unless directed by a police officer

    60. c. Rest Area Ahead

Explanation

51. A yellow and black circular sign with a picture of a truck indicates a designated truck route.

    52. Use high-beam headlights on poorly lit roads and in rural areas without oncoming traffic.

    53. When you see a "DO NOT ENTER" sign, make a U-turn and proceed in the opposite direction.

    54. A red and white triangular sign with the word "YIELD" indicates that you should yield the right-of-way.

    55. A green rectangular sign with white lettering is a guide sign providing directional information.

56. Use parking lights only during nighttime to make your vehicle more visible when parked.

57. A black and yellow circular sign with a picture of a bicycle indicates the presence of a bicycle lane.

58. A white rectangular sign with black lettering and a red circle with a line through it indicates a prohibition, such as "Do Not Enter."

59. Never pass a vehicle stopped at a crosswalk for pedestrians unless directed by a police officer.

60. A blue rectangular sign with white lettering indicates the presence of a rest area ahead.

61. What does a yellow and black circular sign with the word "SLOW" indicate?

a. Slow down and prepare to stop

b. Advisory speed limit

c. No passing zone

d. Merge right

62. When is it appropriate to use your hazard lights while driving?

a. During normal daytime driving

b. When merging onto a highway

c. Only in emergencies to warn other drivers of a potential hazard

d. In well-lit urban areas

63. What does a rectangular white sign with black lettering indicate?

a. Speed Limit

b. Stop Sign Ahead

c. No Parking Zone

d. School Zone Ahead

64. What does a yellow and black circular sign with the word "RAMP" indicate?

a. Hospital Zone Ahead

b. Exit Ramp Ahead

c. Merge Right

d. Rest Area Ahead

65. When are you allowed to turn left at a red traffic light?

a. Only when turning onto a one-way street

b. Never, unless directed by a traffic officer

c. When the way is clear of oncoming traffic and pedestrians

d. Only when there is a green arrow signal

66. What does a blue circular sign with a white symbol indicate?

a. Hospital Zone

b. Informational Sign

c. Mandatory Roundabout Ahead

d. One-Way Traffic

67. When must you stop for a school bus with flashing red lights and a stop sign extended on a divided highway?

a. Never, as a divided highway exempts drivers from stopping

b. Only if you are traveling in the same direction as the bus

c. Always, regardless of the direction of travel

d. Only if you are behind the bus

68. What does a white rectangular sign with black symbols and the word "ONLY" indicate?

a. No Parking Zone

b. Speed Limit

c. Lane Usage

d. Rest Area Ahead

69. What does a yellow and black diamond-shaped sign with a symbol of a truck tipping over indicate?

a. Steep Grade Ahead

b. Truck Rollover Warning

c. Slippery When Wet

d. No Trucks Allowed

70. What does a green and white rectangular sign with the word "MILE" indicate?

a. Mile Marker

b. Speed Limit

c. Exit Ahead

d. Rest Area Ahead

Answers

61. b. Advisory speed limit

62. c. Only in emergencies to warn other drivers of a potential hazard

63. d. School Zone Ahead

64. b. Exit Ramp Ahead

65. a. Only when turning onto a one-way street

66. d. One-Way Traffic

67. c. Always, regardless of the direction of travel
68. c. Lane Usage
69. b. Truck Rollover Warning
70. a. Mile Marker

Explanation

61. A yellow and black circular sign with the word "SLOW" indicates an advisory speed limit.
62. Use hazard lights only in emergencies to warn other drivers of a potential hazard.
63. A rectangular white sign with black lettering typically indicates the presence of a school zone ahead.
64. A yellow and black circular sign with the word "RAMP" indicates an upcoming exit ramp.
65. You are allowed to turn left at a red traffic light only when turning onto a one-way street and the way is clear of oncoming traffic and pedestrians.
66. A blue circular sign with a white symbol generally indicates mandatory actions, such as driving in one-way traffic.
67. Drivers must always stop for a school bus with flashing red lights and a stop sign extended on a divided highway, regardless of the direction of travel.
68. A white rectangular sign with black symbols and the word "ONLY" indicates specific lane usage.
69. A yellow and black diamond-shaped sign with a symbol of a truck tipping over warns of the risk of a truck rollover.
70. A green and white rectangular sign with the word "MILE" indicates a mile marker, providing information about the distance traveled on the road.

71. What does a white rectangular sign with black symbols and the word "EXIT" indicate?
a. Speed Limit
b. No Parking Zone
c. Hospital Zone Ahead
d. Exit Ramp Ahead

72. What does a yellow and black circular sign with a picture of two arrows merging indicate?
a. Merging Traffic
b. Divided Highway Ends
c. Lane Ends
d. No Passing Zone

73. When are you allowed to make a U-turn in a business district?

a. Only at intersections

b. When there are no other vehicles nearby

c. Only at designated U-turn zones

d. Never, unless directed by a police officer

74. What does a green rectangular sign with white lettering indicate?

a. No Parking Zone

b. Informational Sign

c. Guide Sign

d. Rest Area Ahead

75. When should you use your turn signals when changing lanes?

a. After completing the lane change

b. Only when there is heavy traffic

c. Before starting the lane change

d. Only when turning right

76. What does a black and yellow diamond-shaped sign with the word "CROSSBUCK" indicate?

a. Railroad Crossing Ahead

b. Yield Ahead

c. School Zone Ahead

d. Pedestrian Crossing

77. When are you allowed to drive in a bike lane?

a. To pass a slower-moving vehicle

b. When making a right turn

c. Only when there are no bicyclists present

d. During rush hour traffic

78. What does a yellow and black diamond-shaped sign with the word "ROAD WORK" indicate?

a. No Passing Zone

b. Construction Zone Ahead

c. Slippery When Wet

d. Warning - Steep Grade Ahead

79. What does a red and white triangular sign with a red border and the word "ONE WAY" indicate?

a. Warning - Yield Ahead

b. Merge Right

c. One-Way Traffic Only

d. Do Not Enter

80. When should you use your headlights?

a. Only at night

b. During inclement weather or low visibility

c. When driving in well-lit urban areas

d. Only on rural roads

Answers

71. d. Exit Ramp Ahead

72. a. Merging Traffic

73. d. Never, unless directed by a police officer

74. c. Guide Sign

75. c. Before starting the lane change

76. a. Railroad Crossing Ahead

77. b. When making a right turn

78. b. Construction Zone Ahead

79. c. One-Way Traffic Only

80. b. During inclement weather or low visibility

Explanation

71. A white rectangular sign with black symbols and the word "EXIT" indicates an upcoming exit ramp.

72. A yellow and black circular sign with a picture of two arrows merging indicates merging traffic.

73. U-turns in a business district are generally allowed only at intersections unless prohibited by a sign or signal.

74. A green rectangular sign with white lettering is typically a guide sign providing directional information.

75. Use your turn signals before starting the lane change to inform other drivers of your intentions.

76. A black and yellow diamond-shaped sign with the word "CROSSBUCK" indicates a railroad crossing ahead.

77. Drive in a bike lane only when making a right turn.

78. A yellow and black diamond-shaped sign with the word "ROAD WORK" indicates an upcoming construction zone.

79. A red and white triangular sign with a red border and the word "ONE WAY" indicates one-way traffic only.

80. Use headlights during inclement weather or low visibility to enhance visibility for yourself and others on the road.

81. What does a blue circular sign with a white symbol of an "H" indicate?

a. Hospital Zone Ahead

b. Helicopter Landing Zone

c. Handicap Parking Zone

d. Hotel Accommodations Ahead

82. When must you stop for a school bus with flashing red lights and a stop sign extended on a two-lane road?

a. Never, as a two-lane road exempts drivers from stopping

b. Only if you are traveling in the same direction as the bus

c. Always, regardless of the direction of travel

d. Only if you are behind the bus

83. What does a white rectangular sign with black lettering and a red circle with a line through it indicate?

a. No Parking Zone

b. No U-turn

c. No Left Turn

d. Do Not Enter

84. What does a yellow and black circular sign with a picture of a truck tipping over and the word "HAZARDOUS" indicate?

a. Steep Grade Ahead

b. Truck Rollover Warning

c. Slippery When Wet

d. No Trucks Allowed

85. What does a white rectangular sign with black lettering and an orange diamond symbol indicate?

a. Construction Zone Ahead

b. Detour

c. Hospital Zone Ahead

d. No Passing Zone

86. When are you allowed to make a right turn at a red traffic light?

a. Only after coming to a complete stop and yielding to pedestrians and other traffic

b. Never, unless directed by a traffic officer

c. Only when turning onto a one-way street

d. Only during the daytime

87. What does a black and white rectangular sign with the word "STOP" indicate?

a. Yield Ahead

b. Stop Sign Ahead

c. School Zone Ahead

d. Stop Ahead

88. What does a green rectangular sign with white lettering and a white symbol of a bicycle indicate?

a. Bicycle Lane

b. Bicycle Parking

c. No Bicycles Allowed

d. Warning - Bicycles Crossing

89. What does a yellow and black diamond-shaped sign with the word "WARNING" indicate?

a. School Zone Ahead

b. Slippery When Wet

c. Merge Right

d. Detour Ahead

90. When should you use your vehicle's horn?

a. To express frustration or annoyance

b. To signal your approval of another driver's actions

c. Only in emergencies to avoid a collision

d. When driving in well-lit urban areas

Answers

81. b. Helicopter Landing Zone

82. c. Always, regardless of the direction of travel

83. b. No U-turn

84. b. Truck Rollover Warning

85. a. Construction Zone Ahead

86. a. Only after coming to a complete stop and yielding to pedestrians and other traffic

87. b. Stop Sign Ahead

88. a. Bicycle Lane

89. b. Slippery When Wet

90. c. Only in emergencies to avoid a collision

Explanation

81. A blue circular sign with a white symbol of an "H" indicates a helicopter landing zone.

82. Drivers must always stop for a school bus with flashing red lights and a stop sign extended on a two-lane road, regardless of the direction of travel.

83. A white rectangular sign with black lettering and a red circle with a line through it indicates a prohibition, such as "No U-turn."

84. A yellow and black circular sign with a picture of a truck tipping over and the word "HAZARDOUS" warns of a hazardous condition, such as a potential truck rollover.

85. A white rectangular sign with black lettering and an orange diamond symbol indicates a construction zone ahead.

86. You are allowed to make a right turn at a red traffic light only after coming to a complete stop and yielding to pedestrians and other traffic.

87. A black and white rectangular sign with the word "STOP" indicates an upcoming stop sign.

88. A green rectangular sign with white lettering and a white symbol of a bicycle indicates a designated bicycle lane.

89. A yellow and black diamond-shaped sign with the word "WARNING" indicates a general warning about potential hazards ahead.

90. Use your vehicle's horn only in emergencies to avoid a collision.

91. What does a yellow and black circular sign with a picture of a deer and the word "CROSSING" indicate?

a. Warning - School Zone

b. No Deer Hunting Zone

c. Deer Crossing

d. Slippery When Wet

92. When must you use your headlights?

a. Only in well-lit urban areas

b. During daytime to enhance visibility

c. Only at night or when visibility is reduced

d. Only when approaching a traffic signal

93. What does a blue rectangular sign with white lettering and a white symbol of a wheelchair indicate?

a. Handicap Parking Zone

b. Hospital Zone

c. School Zone

d. Emergency Vehicle Parking

94. When are you allowed to pass a vehicle on the left using a center turn lane?

a. Only in designated passing zones

b. When the vehicle in front is turning left

c. When there is oncoming traffic in the opposite lane

d. Never, unless directed by a police officer

95. What does a red and white triangular sign with the word "SLOW" indicate?

a. Advisory speed limit

b. School Zone Ahead

c. Merge Ahead

d. Right-of-Way Ahead

96. What does a black and white rectangular sign with the word "DO NOT ENTER" indicate?

a. Merge Right

b. One-Way Traffic

c. No Passing Zone

d. Do Not Pass

97. When is it appropriate to use your vehicle's high-beam headlights in the presence of oncoming traffic?

a. Always, for better visibility

b. Only in rural areas with no other vehicles around

c. Only when passing another vehicle

d. Never, to avoid blinding other drivers

98. What does a yellow and black circular sign with the word "CAUTION" indicate?

a. School Zone Ahead

b. Slippery When Wet

c. No Passing Zone

d. Pedestrian Crossing

99. What does a white rectangular sign with black symbols and the word "LANE" indicate?

a. No Passing Zone

b. Speed Limit

c. Lane Usage

d. Construction Zone Ahead

100. What does a red and white triangular sign with a red border and the word "YIELD" indicate?

a. Stop Ahead

b. Warning - Stop Ahead

c. Right-of-Way Ahead

d. Yield the Right-of-Way

Answers

91. c. Deer Crossing

92. c. Only at night or when visibility is reduced

93. a. Handicap Parking Zone

94. b. When the vehicle in front is turning left

95. a. Advisory speed limit

96. b. One-Way Traffic

97. d. Never, to avoid blinding other drivers

98. b. Slippery When Wet

99. c. Lane Usage

100.   d. Yield the Right-of-Way

Explanation

91. A yellow and black circular sign with a picture of a deer and the word "CROSSING" indicates a deer crossing warning.

92. Use headlights only at night or when visibility is reduced to enhance visibility for yourself and others on the road.

93. A blue rectangular sign with white lettering and a white symbol of a wheelchair indicates a handicap parking zone.

94. Pass a vehicle on the left using a center turn lane only when the vehicle in front is turning left.

95. A red and white triangular sign with the word "SLOW" indicates an advisory speed limit.

96. A black and white rectangular sign with the word "DO NOT ENTER" indicates one-way traffic, and entering is prohibited.

97. Use high-beam headlights sparingly, especially in the presence of oncoming traffic, to avoid blinding other drivers.

98. A yellow and black circular sign with the word "CAUTION" indicates a general warning about potential hazards ahead.

99. A white rectangular sign with black symbols and the word "LANE" indicates specific lane usage.

100. A red and white triangular sign with a red border and the word "YIELD" indicates that you should yield the right-of-way.

Practice Test 2: Traffic Laws and Regulations

1. What does a red and white triangular sign with a red border and the word "STOP" indicate?

    a. Yield the Right-of-Way

    b. Merge Ahead

    c. Stop Ahead

    d. Right-of-Way Ahead

2. What does a yellow and black circular sign with the word "SPEED LIMIT" indicate?

    a. Advisory speed limit

    b. No Passing Zone

    c. Maximum Speed Allowed

    d. Construction Zone Ahead

3. When are you allowed to make a U-turn at an intersection with a traffic signal?

    a. Only if there is a "U-Turn Permitted" sign

    b. When the way is clear of oncoming traffic and pedestrians

    c. Only during nighttime

    d. Never, unless directed by a traffic officer

4. What does a rectangular white sign with black lettering and a red circle with a line through it indicate?

    a. No Left Turn

    b. No Parking Zone

    c. Do Not Enter

    d. No U-turn

5. What does a blue rectangular sign with white lettering and a white symbol of a hospital indicate?

    a. Hospital Zone

    b. Informational Sign

    c. Emergency Parking Only

    d. No Parking Zone

6. When are you required to use your vehicle's headlights?

a. Only during nighttime

b. In well-lit urban areas

c. Only during inclement weather

d. Only when approaching a stop sign

7. What does a yellow and black circular sign with a picture of a school bus and the words "STOP AHEAD" indicate?

a. School Zone Ahead

b. Stop Sign Ahead

c. Yield Ahead

d. Stop for School Buses Ahead

8. When must you stop for a school bus with flashing red lights and a stop sign extended on a two-lane road?

a. Never, as a two-lane road exempts drivers from stopping

b. Only if you are traveling in the same direction as the bus

c. Always, regardless of the direction of travel

d. Only if you are behind the bus

9. What does a yellow and black diamond-shaped sign with the word "RAILROAD" indicate?

a. Construction Zone Ahead

b. Railroad Crossing Ahead

c. Slippery When Wet

d. Warning - Steep Grade Ahead

10. When are you allowed to pass a vehicle on the right?

a. Only in designated passing zones

b. When the vehicle is making a left turn

c. When the vehicle is slowing down for a yellow light

d. Never, unless driving on a one-way street

Answers:

1. c. Stop Ahead

2. c. Maximum Speed Allowed

3. a. Only if there is a "U-Turn Permitted" sign

4. c. Do Not Enter

5. a. Hospital Zone

6. a. Only during nighttime

7. d. Stop for School Buses Ahead

8. c. Always, regardless of the direction of travel

9. b. Railroad Crossing Ahead

10. d. Never, unless driving on a one-way street

Explanation:

1. A red and white triangular sign with the word "STOP" indicates an upcoming stop sign.

2. A yellow and black circular sign with the word "SPEED LIMIT" indicates the maximum speed allowed in that area.

3. U-turns at intersections with traffic signals are generally allowed only if there is a "U-Turn Permitted" sign.

4. A rectangular white sign with black lettering and a red circle with a line through it indicates a prohibition, such as "Do Not Enter."

5. A blue rectangular sign with white lettering and a white symbol of a hospital indicates the presence of a hospital zone.

6. Use headlights only during nighttime to enhance visibility for yourself and others on the road.

7. A yellow and black circular sign with a picture of a school bus and the words "STOP AHEAD" indicates that you should be prepared to stop for school buses ahead.

8. Drivers must always stop for a school bus with flashing red lights and a stop sign extended on a two-lane road, regardless of the direction of travel.

9. A yellow and black diamond-shaped sign with the word "RAILROAD" warns of an upcoming railroad crossing.

10. Passing a vehicle on the right is generally allowed only when driving on a one-way street.

11. What does a yellow and black diamond-shaped sign with the word "CAUTION" indicate?

    a. School Zone Ahead

    b. Slippery When Wet

    c. No Passing Zone

    d. Pedestrian Crossing

12. What does a white rectangular sign with black symbols and the words "LANE ENDS" indicate?

    a. Lane Reduction Ahead

    b. No Passing Zone

    c. Lane Usage

    d. Merge Left

13. When are you required to use your turn signals?

    a. Only when turning left

    b. Only when turning right

    c. Before changing lanes or making a turn

    d. Only during inclement weather

14. What does a red and white triangular sign with the word "YIELD" indicate?

    a. Stop Ahead

    b. Warning - Stop Ahead

    c. Right-of-Way Ahead

    d. Yield the Right-of-Way

15. When is it appropriate to use your hazard lights while driving?

    a. During normal daytime driving

    b. When merging onto a highway

    c. Only in emergencies to warn other drivers of a potential hazard

    d. In well-lit urban areas

16. What does a green rectangular sign with white lettering and a white symbol of a bicycle indicate?

    a. Bicycle Lane

    b. Bicycle Parking

    c. No Bicycles Allowed

    d. Warning - Bicycles Crossing

17. When must you yield the right-of-way to pedestrians?

    a. Only when crossing at marked crosswalks

    b. Only if the pedestrian is in a hurry

    c. Always, at intersections and crosswalks

d. Never, unless directed by a police officer

18. What does a yellow and black circular sign with the word "ONE WAY" indicate?

   a. One-Way Traffic Only

   b. Merge Right

   c. No Passing Zone

   d. Do Not Enter

19. When are you allowed to pass a school bus with flashing red lights and a stop sign extended on a divided highway?

   a. Never, as a divided highway exempts drivers from stopping

   b. Only if you are traveling in the same direction as the bus

   c. Always, regardless of the direction of travel

   d. Only if you are behind the bus

20. What does a blue circular sign with a white symbol of an "H" indicate?

   a. Hospital Zone Ahead

   b. Helicopter Landing Zone

   c. Handicap Parking Zone

   d. Hotel Accommodations Ahead

Answers:

11. b. Slippery When Wet

12. d. Merge Left

13. c. Before changing lanes or making a turn

14. d. Yield the Right-of-Way

15. c. Only in emergencies to warn other drivers of a potential hazard

16. a. Bicycle Lane

17. c. Always, at intersections and crosswalks

18. a. One-Way Traffic Only

19. a. Never, as a divided highway exempts drivers from stopping

20. b. Helicopter Landing Zone

Explanation:

11. A yellow and black diamond-shaped sign with the word "CAUTION" indicates a general warning about potential hazards, such as slippery conditions.

12. A white rectangular sign with black symbols and the words "LANE ENDS" indicates that the lane you are in will soon end, and you should prepare to merge left.

13. Use your turn signals before changing lanes or making a turn to inform other drivers of your intentions.

14. A red and white triangular sign with the word "YIELD" indicates that you should yield the right-of-way to other vehicles.

15. Use hazard lights only in emergencies to warn other drivers of a potential hazard.

16. A green rectangular sign with white lettering and a white symbol of a bicycle indicates a designated bicycle lane.

17. Drivers must always yield the right-of-way to pedestrians at intersections and crosswalks.

18. A yellow and black circular sign with the word "ONE WAY" indicates that the road is for one-way traffic only.

19. Never pass a school bus with flashing red lights and a stop sign extended on a divided highway, as drivers on the opposite side are also required to stop.

20. A blue circular sign with a white symbol of an "H" indicates a helicopter landing zone.

21. What does a yellow and black circular sign with a picture of a deer and the words "CAUTION - DEER CROSSING" indicate?
   a. Slippery When Wet
   b. No Deer Hunting Zone
   c. Deer Crossing
   d. Warning - Animals Ahead

22. What does a red rectangular sign with white lettering and the word "FIRE" indicate?
   a. Fire Station Ahead
   b. Emergency Exit
   c. No Open Flames Allowed
   d. Fire Hydrant Zone

23. When approaching a railroad crossing with flashing red lights, what should you do?
   a. Proceed with caution, as the lights may be malfunctioning
   b. Stop and wait for the lights to stop flashing before crossing

c. Speed up to clear the tracks quickly

d. Honk your horn to warn approaching trains

24. What does a green and white rectangular sign with the words "EXIT ONLY" indicate?

    a. Rest Area Ahead

    b. Exit Ramp Ahead

    c. Lane Usage

    d. Detour Ahead

25. When are you allowed to use your cell phone while driving?

    a. Only when using hands-free devices

    b. Only during daytime hours

    c. When stopped at a red traffic light

    d. Never, unless reporting an emergency

26. What does a yellow and black diamond-shaped sign with a picture of a person swinging a flag indicate?

    a. Road Work Ahead

    b. Pedestrian Crossing

    c. School Zone Ahead

    d. Flag Person Ahead

27. What does a yellow and black circular sign with a picture of a person walking and the words "PEDESTRIAN CROSSING" indicate?

    a. School Zone Ahead

    b. Slippery When Wet

    c. Yield to Pedestrians

    d. No Walking Zone

28. When are you required to use snow chains on your tires?

    a. Only during heavy snowfall

    b. When driving in mountainous areas where posted

    c. Only on icy roads

    d. Never, as they are not required by law

29. What does a yellow and black circular sign with a picture of a truck and the words "TRUCKS ENTERING HIGHWAY" indicate?

    a. Truck Rollover Warning

    b. No Trucks Allowed

    c. Steep Grade Ahead

    d. Merge Right

30. When must you use your vehicle's low-beam headlights?

    a. Only in well-lit urban areas

    b. During daytime to enhance visibility

    c. Only during inclement weather or when visibility is reduced

    d. Never, unless driving on a rural road

Answers:

21. c. Deer Crossing

22. a. Fire Station Ahead

23. b. Stop and wait for the lights to stop flashing before crossing

24. b. Exit Ramp Ahead

25. d. Never, unless reporting an emergency

26. d. Flag Person Ahead

27. c. Yield to Pedestrians

28. b. When driving in mountainous areas where posted

29. a. Truck Rollover Warning

30. c. Only during inclement weather or when visibility is reduced

Explanation:

21. A yellow and black circular sign with a picture of a deer and the words "CAUTION - DEER CROSSING" indicates that you should be cautious of deer crossing the road.

22. A red rectangular sign with white lettering and the word "FIRE" indicates the presence of a fire station.

23. When approaching a railroad crossing with flashing red lights, you must stop and wait for the lights to stop flashing before crossing.

24. A green and white rectangular sign with the words "EXIT ONLY" indicates that the upcoming lane is an exit lane.

25. In most places, using a cell phone while driving is prohibited, except in emergencies.

26. A yellow and black diamond-shaped sign with a picture of a person swinging a flag indicates the presence of a flag person ahead, typically in construction zones.

27. A yellow and black circular sign with a picture of a person walking and the words "PEDESTRIAN CROSSING" indicates that you should yield to pedestrians in the marked crossing.

28. Use snow chains on your tires when driving in mountainous areas where posted.

29. A yellow and black circular sign with a picture of a truck and the words "TRUCKS ENTERING HIGHWAY" warns that trucks may be entering the highway.

30. Use your vehicle's low-beam headlights during inclement weather or when visibility is reduced to avoid blinding other drivers.

31. What does a white rectangular sign with black lettering and a red circle with a line through it indicate?

   a. No Parking Zone

   b. No U-turn

   c. No Passing Zone

   d. Do Not Enter

32. When is it permissible to exceed the posted speed limit?

   a. Only when passing another vehicle

   b. During daylight hours

   c. When driving on a highway

   d. Never, unless directed by a traffic officer

33. What does a yellow and black circular sign with the words "RAILROAD CROSSING AHEAD" indicate?

   a. Slippery When Wet

   b. School Zone Ahead

   c. Railroad Crossing Ahead

   d. Warning - Steep Grade Ahead

34. When must you use your vehicle's headlights?

   a. Only during nighttime

b. During daytime in well-lit urban areas

c. Only in inclement weather or low visibility

d. Only when there are other vehicles around

35. What does a yellow and black diamond-shaped sign with the word "WARNING" indicate?

a. School Zone Ahead

b. Detour Ahead

c. Slippery When Wet

d. Merge Right

36. What does a blue circular sign with a white symbol of a wheelchair indicate?

a. Handicap Parking Zone

b. Hospital Zone

c. School Zone

d. Disabled Access Ahead

37. When are you allowed to pass a vehicle on the right on a multilane highway?

a. Only if the vehicle is turning left

b. When the vehicle in front is moving too slowly

c. Only during rush hour traffic

d. Never, unless directed by a police officer

38. What does a yellow and black circular sign with a picture of two arrows merging indicate?

a. Merging Traffic

b. Divided Highway Ends

c. Lane Ends

d. No Passing Zone

39. What does a red and white triangular sign with the word "SLOW" indicate?

a. Advisory speed limit

b. School Zone Ahead

c. Merge Ahead

d. Right-of-Way Ahead

40. What does a green rectangular sign with white lettering and a white symbol of a bicycle indicate?

   a. Bicycle Lane

   b. Bicycle Parking

   c. No Bicycles Allowed

   d. Warning - Bicycles Crossing

Answers:

31. d. Do Not Enter

32. d. Never, unless directed by a traffic officer

33. c. Railroad Crossing Ahead

34. c. Only in inclement weather or low visibility

35. c. Slippery When Wet

36. a. Handicap Parking Zone

37. d. Never, unless directed by a police officer

38. a. Merging Traffic

39. a. Advisory speed limit

40. a. Bicycle Lane

Explanation:

31. A white rectangular sign with black lettering and a red circle with a line through it indicates a prohibition, such as "Do Not Enter."

32. Exceeding the posted speed limit is generally not allowed, except when directed by a traffic officer.

33. A yellow and black circular sign with the words "RAILROAD CROSSING AHEAD" warns of an upcoming railroad crossing.

34. Use headlights only in inclement weather or low visibility to enhance visibility for yourself and others on the road.

35. A yellow and black diamond-shaped sign with the word "WARNING" indicates a general warning about potential hazards, such as slippery conditions.

36. A blue circular sign with a white symbol of a wheelchair indicates a handicap parking zone.

37. Passing a vehicle on the right on a multilane highway is generally not allowed unless directed by a police officer.

38. A yellow and black circular sign with a picture of two arrows merging indicates merging traffic.

39. A red and white triangular sign with the word "SLOW" indicates an advisory speed limit.

40. A green rectangular sign with white lettering and a white symbol of a bicycle indicates a designated bicycle lane.

41. What does a red and white triangular sign with the words "SHARE THE ROAD" indicate?
   a. Pedestrian Crossing Ahead
   b. Bicycles Allowed
   c. Yield Ahead
   d. Right-of-Way Ahead

42. When must you use your vehicle's turn signals?
   a. Only when turning left
   b. Only when turning right
   c. Before changing lanes or making a turn
   d. Only during nighttime

43. What does a yellow and black circular sign with a picture of a person walking and the words "SCHOOL CROSSING" indicate?
   a. School Zone Ahead
   b. Pedestrian Crossing
   c. Yield to Pedestrians
   d. No Walking Zone

44. When are you allowed to make a left turn at a red traffic light?
   a. Only after coming to a complete stop and yielding to pedestrians and other traffic
   b. Never, unless directed by a traffic officer
   c. Only during nighttime
   d. Only when turning onto a one-way street

45. What does a white rectangular sign with black lettering and a picture of a truck tipping over indicate?
   a. Slippery When Wet
   b. No Trucks Allowed
   c. Truck Rollover Warning
   d. Merge Right

46. What does a blue rectangular sign with white lettering and a white symbol of a gas pump indicate?

   a. Gas Station Ahead

   b. Rest Area Ahead

   c. Fueling Station for Emergency Vehicles

   d. No Gasoline Service

47. What does a yellow and black diamond-shaped sign with a picture of a deer and the words "WATCH FOR DEER" indicate?

   a. Deer Crossing

   b. No Deer Hunting Zone

   c. Warning - Animals Ahead

   d. Slippery When Wet

48. What does a red rectangular sign with white lettering and the word "NO TURN ON RED" indicate?

   a. Right-of-Way Ahead

   b. Stop Ahead

   c. No Right Turn on Red

   d. No Left Turn on Red

49. When are you required to come to a complete stop at a stop sign?

   a. Only when other vehicles are present

   b. Only when making a right turn

   c. Always, regardless of other traffic or pedestrians

   d. Only when turning left

50. What does a green and white rectangular sign with the words "EXIT 25" indicate?

   a. Rest Area Ahead

   b. Exit Ramp Ahead

   c. Lane Usage

   d. Detour Ahead

Answers:

41. b. Bicycles Allowed

42. c. Before changing lanes or making a turn

43. b. Pedestrian Crossing

44. a. Only after coming to a complete stop and yielding to pedestrians and other traffic

45. c. Truck Rollover Warning

46. a. Gas Station Ahead

47. c. Warning - Animals Ahead

48. c. No Right Turn on Red

49. c. Always, regardless of other traffic or pedestrians

50. b. Exit Ramp Ahead

Explanation:

41. A red and white triangular sign with the words "SHARE THE ROAD" indicates that bicycles are allowed and that drivers should be aware of cyclists.

42. Use your vehicle's turn signals before changing lanes or making a turn to inform other drivers of your intentions.

43. A yellow and black circular sign with a picture of a person walking and the words "SCHOOL CROSSING" indicates a marked school crossing where drivers should yield to pedestrians.

44. Make a left turn at a red traffic light only after coming to a complete stop and yielding to pedestrians and other traffic, unless a sign prohibits it.

45. A white rectangular sign with black lettering and a picture of a truck tipping over indicates a warning about the potential for a truck rollover.

46. A blue rectangular sign with white lettering and a white symbol of a gas pump indicates the presence of a gas station.

47. A yellow and black diamond-shaped sign with a picture of a deer and the words "WATCH FOR DEER" warns drivers to be cautious and watch for deer in the area.

48. A red rectangular sign with white lettering and the word "NO TURN ON RED" indicates that making a right turn on a red traffic light is not allowed.

49. Come to a complete stop at a stop sign always, regardless of other traffic or pedestrians, before proceeding.

50. A green and white rectangular sign with the words "EXIT 25" indicates that Exit 25 is approaching on the highway.

51. What does a yellow and black circular sign with a picture of a bicycle and the words "BIKE LANE" indicate?

   a. No Bicycles Allowed

b. Bicycle Parking Zone

c. Shared Lane for Bicycles and Vehicles

d. Designated Bicycle Lane

52. When are you required to use your headlights?

a. Only during daytime hours

b. Only at night or when visibility is reduced

c. Only when driving on a highway

d. Only in construction zones

53. What does a white rectangular sign with black lettering and a red circle with a line through it indicate?

a. No Parking Zone

b. No U-turn

c. No Passing Zone

d. Do Not Enter

54. When must you use snow chains on your tires?

a. Only during heavy snowfall

b. When driving in mountainous areas where posted

c. Only on icy roads

d. Never, as they are not required by law

55. What does a yellow and black diamond-shaped sign with the words "LANE ENDS MERGE LEFT" indicate?

a. Lane Reduction Ahead

b. No Passing Zone

c. Merging Traffic

d. Divided Highway Ends

56. What does a red and white triangular sign with the word "YIELD" indicate?

a. Stop Ahead

b. Warning - Stop Ahead

c. Right-of-Way Ahead

d. Yield the Right-of-Way

57. When are you allowed to pass a vehicle on the right?

    a. Only in designated passing zones

    b. When the vehicle is making a left turn

    c. When the vehicle is slowing down for a yellow light

    d. Never, unless driving on a one-way street

58. What does a blue circular sign with a white symbol of a water droplet indicate?

    a. Rest Area Ahead

    b. Water Station Ahead

    c. Water Conservation Zone

    d. Flood Area Ahead

59. What does a yellow and black circular sign with a picture of a truck and the words "HILL BLOCKING VIEW" indicate?

    a. Steep Grade Ahead

    b. Trucks Entering Highway

    c. Warning - Blind Intersection

    d. Slippery When Wet

60. When must you use your vehicle's high-beam headlights?

    a. Only in well-lit urban areas

    b. Only at night and in rural areas with no other vehicles around

    c. Only during inclement weather or when visibility is reduced

    d. Never, to avoid blinding other drivers

Answers:

51. d. Designated Bicycle Lane

52. b. Only at night or when visibility is reduced

53. d. Do Not Enter

54. b. When driving in mountainous areas where posted

55. a. Lane Reduction Ahead

56. d. Yield the Right-of-Way

57. d. Never, unless driving on a one-way street

58. d. Flood Area Ahead

59. c. Warning - Blind Intersection

60. c. Only during inclement weather or when visibility is reduced

Explanation:

51. A yellow and black circular sign with a picture of a bicycle and the words "BIKE LANE" indicates the presence of a designated bicycle lane.

52. Use headlights only at night or when visibility is reduced to enhance visibility for yourself and others on the road.

53. A white rectangular sign with black lettering and a red circle with a line through it indicates a prohibition, such as "Do Not Enter."

54. Use snow chains on your tires when driving in mountainous areas where posted.

55. A yellow and black diamond-shaped sign with the words "LANE ENDS MERGE LEFT" indicates that the lane is ending, and drivers should prepare to merge left.

56. A red and white triangular sign with the word "YIELD" indicates that you should yield the right-of-way to other vehicles.

57. Passing a vehicle on the right is generally not allowed, unless driving on a one-way street.

58. A blue circular sign with a white symbol of a water droplet indicates a flood area ahead.

59. A yellow and black circular sign with a picture of a truck and the words "HILL BLOCKING VIEW" indicates a warning about a hill blocking the view, often at intersections.

60. Use high-beam headlights only during inclement weather or when visibility is reduced to avoid blinding other drivers.

61. What does a yellow and black circular sign with the words "KEEP RIGHT" indicate?

    a. No Passing Zone

    b. Merge Right

    c. Divided Highway Ends

    d. Keep Right Except to Pass

62. When are you required to use your vehicle's hazard lights?

    a. During normal daytime driving

    b. When merging onto a highway

    c. Only in emergencies to warn other drivers of a potential hazard

    d. In well-lit urban areas

63. What does a blue rectangular sign with white lettering and a white symbol of an airplane indicate?

a. Airport Zone Ahead

b. Rest Area Ahead

c. No Flying Zone

d. Flyover Ramp Ahead

64. When approaching a stopped emergency vehicle with flashing lights on a multilane road, what should you do?

a. Maintain your speed and proceed with caution

b. Slow down and move to a non-adjacent lane if possible

c. Speed up to pass quickly

d. Honk your horn to alert the emergency personnel

65. What does a yellow and black diamond-shaped sign with a picture of a truck tipping over indicate?

a. Slippery When Wet

b. Truck Rollover Warning

c. No Trucks Allowed

d. Merge Right

66. What does a white rectangular sign with black lettering and a red circle with a line through it indicate?

a. No Parking Zone

b. No U-turn

c. No Passing Zone

d. Do Not Enter

67. When are you allowed to make a U-turn at an intersection with a traffic signal?

a. Only if there is a "U-Turn Permitted" sign

b. When the way is clear of oncoming traffic and pedestrians

c. Only during nighttime

d. Never, unless directed by a traffic officer

68. What does a yellow and black circular sign with a picture of a person walking and the words "PEDESTRIAN CROSSING" indicate?

a. School Zone Ahead

b. Slippery When Wet

c. Yield to Pedestrians

d. No Walking Zone

69. When are you allowed to pass a school bus with flashing red lights and a stop sign extended on a two-lane road?

a. Never, as a two-lane road exempts drivers from stopping

b. Only if you are traveling in the same direction as the bus

c. Always, regardless of the direction of travel

d. Only if you are behind the bus

70. What does a green and white rectangular sign with the words "KEEP CLEAR" indicate?

a. Right-of-Way Ahead

b. Keep Right Except to Pass

c. Do Not Block Intersection

d. No Stopping Zone

Answers:

61. d. Keep Right Except to Pass

62. c. Only in emergencies to warn other drivers of a potential hazard

63. a. Airport Zone Ahead

64. b. Slow down and move to a non-adjacent lane if possible

65. b. Truck Rollover Warning

66. d. Do Not Enter

67. b. When the way is clear of oncoming traffic and pedestrians

68. c. Yield to Pedestrians

69. b. Only if you are traveling in the same direction as the bus

70. c. Do Not Block Intersection

Explanation:

61. A yellow and black circular sign with the words "KEEP RIGHT" indicates that drivers should keep right except to pass.

62. Use hazard lights only in emergencies to warn other drivers of a potential hazard.

63. A blue rectangular sign with white lettering and a white symbol of an airplane indicates the presence of an airport zone.

64. When approaching a stopped emergency vehicle with flashing lights on a multilane road, slow down and move to a non-adjacent lane if possible.

65. A yellow and black diamond-shaped sign with a picture of a truck tipping over indicates a warning about the potential for a truck rollover.

66. A white rectangular sign with black lettering and a red circle with a line through it indicates a prohibition, such as "Do Not Enter."

67. U-turns at intersections with traffic signals are generally allowed when the way is clear of oncoming traffic and pedestrians.

68. A yellow and black circular sign with a picture of a person walking and the words "PEDESTRIAN CROSSING" indicates that you should yield to pedestrians in the marked crossing.

69. Pass a school bus with flashing red lights and a stop sign extended on a two-lane road only if you are traveling in the same direction as the bus.

70. A green and white rectangular sign with the words "KEEP CLEAR" indicates that drivers should not block the intersection and keep it clear for other traffic.

71. What does a yellow and black circular sign with a picture of a person holding a flag and the words "FLAGGER AHEAD" indicate?
   a. School Zone Ahead
   b. Flag Person Ahead
   c. Road Work Ahead
   d. No Passing Zone

72. When are you required to stop for a school bus with flashing red lights on a divided highway?
   a. Always, regardless of the number of lanes
   b. Only when traveling in the same direction as the bus
   c. Never, as divided highways exempt drivers from stopping
   d. Only when the bus is unloading children

73. What does a yellow and black diamond-shaped sign with the words "LANE ENDS MERGE LEFT" indicate?
   a. Divided Highway Ends
   b. Lane Reduction Ahead

c. Merging Traffic

d. No Passing Zone

74. When approaching a roundabout, what should you do?

   a. Speed up to enter the roundabout quickly

   b. Yield to vehicles already in the roundabout and enter when safe

   c. Honk your horn to alert other drivers

   d. Always make a complete stop before entering the roundabout

75. What does a yellow and black circular sign with a picture of a deer and the words "WATCH FOR DEER" indicate?

   a. Warning - Animals Ahead

   b. No Deer Hunting Zone

   c. Slippery When Wet

   d. Deer Crossing

76. What does a red rectangular sign with white lettering and the words "DO NOT ENTER" indicate?

   a. No U-turn

   b. No Passing Zone

   c. Divided Highway Ends

   d. Wrong Way

77. When are you allowed to pass a vehicle on the right on a two-lane road?

   a. Only in designated passing zones

   b. When the vehicle is turning left

   c. Only during rush hour traffic

   d. Never, unless directed by a police officer

78. What does a yellow and black circular sign with a picture of a pedestrian and the words "CROSSWALK" indicate?

   a. No Walking Zone

   b. Yield to Pedestrians

   c. School Zone Ahead

   d. Slippery When Wet

79. When are you allowed to use your vehicle's horn?

   a. Only during daytime hours

   b. To alert other drivers of your presence or to avoid a collision

   c. Only in well-lit urban areas

   d. Only during inclement weather

80. What does a green rectangular sign with white lettering and a white symbol of a hospital indicate?

   a. Hospital Zone Ahead

   b. Rest Area Ahead

   c. Emergency Services Ahead

   d. Medical Parking Only

Answers:

71. b. Flag Person Ahead

72. b. Only when traveling in the same direction as the bus

73. b. Lane Reduction Ahead

74. b. Yield to vehicles already in the roundabout and enter when safe

75. a. Warning - Animals Ahead

76. d. Wrong Way

77. b. When the vehicle is turning left

78. b. Yield to Pedestrians

79. b. To alert other drivers of your presence or to avoid a collision

80. a. Hospital Zone Ahead

Explanation:

71. A yellow and black circular sign with a picture of a person holding a flag and the words "FLAGGER AHEAD" indicates the presence of a flag person ahead, typically in road work zones.

72. Stop for a school bus with flashing red lights on a divided highway only when traveling in the same direction as the bus.

73. A yellow and black diamond-shaped sign with the words "LANE ENDS MERGE LEFT" indicates that the lane is ending, and drivers should prepare to merge left.

74. When approaching a roundabout, yield to vehicles already in the roundabout and enter when it's safe to do so.

75. A yellow and black circular sign with a picture of a deer and the words "WATCH FOR DEER" warns drivers to be cautious and watch for deer in the area.

76. A red rectangular sign with white lettering and the words "DO NOT ENTER" indicates that entering the road or highway is prohibited.

77. Passing a vehicle on the right on a two-lane road is allowed when the vehicle in front is turning left.

78. A yellow and black circular sign with a picture of a pedestrian and the words "CROSSWALK" indicates the presence of a marked crosswalk, and drivers should yield to pedestrians.

79. Use your vehicle's horn to alert other drivers of your presence or to avoid a collision.

80. A green rectangular sign with white lettering and a white symbol of a hospital indicates the presence of a hospital zone ahead.

81. What does a blue rectangular sign with white lettering and a white symbol of a person on a wheelchair indicate?

    a. Handicap Parking Zone

    b. Hospital Zone Ahead

    c. Disabled Access Ahead

    d. Medical Parking Only

82. When are you required to dim your vehicle's high-beam headlights?

    a. Only in well-lit urban areas

    b. Only in inclement weather or when visibility is reduced

    c. When approaching an oncoming vehicle within 500 feet

    d. Never, to ensure maximum visibility

83. What does a red and white triangular sign with the words "STOP AHEAD" indicate?

    a. Right-of-Way Ahead

    b. Stop Sign Ahead

    c. Warning - Stop Ahead

    d. No Stopping Zone

84. When are you allowed to make a left turn at a red traffic light?

    a. Only after coming to a complete stop and yielding to pedestrians and other traffic

    b. Only during nighttime hours

    c. Only when turning onto a one-way street

d. Never, unless directed by a traffic officer

85. What does a yellow and black diamond-shaped sign with the words "DIVIDED HIGHWAY ENDS" indicate?
   a. Merging Traffic
   b. No Passing Zone
   c. Lane Reduction Ahead
   d. End of Divided Highway

86. What does a red rectangular sign with white lettering and the words "DO NOT PASS" indicate?
   a. No Passing Zone
   b. No Passing Allowed
   c. No Passing on Left
   d. Divided Highway Ends

87. When must you use your vehicle's headlights?
   a. Only during nighttime hours
   b. Only during inclement weather or when visibility is reduced
   c. Only in construction zones
   d. Only when there are other vehicles around

88. What does a yellow and black circular sign with a picture of a traffic signal and the words "SIGNAL AHEAD" indicate?
   a. Stop Sign Ahead
   b. Yield Sign Ahead
   c. Traffic Signal Ahead
   d. Warning - Intersection Ahead

89. When are you allowed to use your vehicle's hazard lights?
   a. Only during normal daytime driving
   b. Only in emergencies to warn other drivers of a potential hazard
   c. Always, to increase visibility
   d. Only during nighttime

90. What does a blue rectangular sign with white lettering and a white symbol of a person on a bicycle indicate?

    a. Bicycle Lane

    b. Share the Road with Bicycles

    c. No Bicycles Allowed

    d. Bicycle Parking

Answers:

81. c. Disabled Access Ahead

82. c. When approaching an oncoming vehicle within 500 feet

83. c. Warning - Stop Ahead

84. a. Only after coming to a complete stop and yielding to pedestrians and other traffic

85. d. End of Divided Highway

86. a. No Passing Zone

87. b. Only during inclement weather or when visibility is reduced

88. c. Traffic Signal Ahead

89. b. Only in emergencies to warn other drivers of a potential hazard

90. b. Share the Road with Bicycles

Explanation:

81. A blue rectangular sign with white lettering and a white symbol of a person on a wheelchair indicates disabled access ahead.

82. Dim your vehicle's high-beam headlights when approaching an oncoming vehicle within 500 feet to avoid blinding the oncoming driver.

83. A red and white triangular sign with the words "STOP AHEAD" warns drivers that a stop sign is approaching.

84. Make a left turn at a red traffic light only after coming to a complete stop and yielding to pedestrians and other traffic, unless a sign prohibits it.

85. A yellow and black diamond-shaped sign with the words "DIVIDED HIGHWAY ENDS" indicates the end of a divided highway.

86. A red rectangular sign with white lettering and the words "DO NOT PASS" indicates a prohibition on passing in the specified area.

87. Use headlights during inclement weather or when visibility is reduced to enhance visibility for yourself and others on the road.

88. A yellow and black circular sign with a picture of a traffic signal and the words "SIGNAL AHEAD" indicates that a traffic signal is approaching.

89. Use hazard lights only in emergencies to warn other drivers of a potential hazard.

90. A blue rectangular sign with white lettering and a white symbol of a person on a bicycle indicates that drivers should share the road with bicycles.

91. What does a white rectangular sign with black lettering and a red circle with a line through it indicate?

   a. No Parking Zone

   b. No U-turn

   c. Do Not Enter

   d. No Passing Zone

92. When are you allowed to use your vehicle's horn?

   a. Only during daytime hours

   b. To alert other drivers of your presence or to avoid a collision

   c. Only in well-lit urban areas

   d. Only during inclement weather

93. What does a yellow and black circular sign with a picture of a person walking and the words "CROSSWALK" indicate?

   a. No Walking Zone

   b. School Zone Ahead

   c. Yield to Pedestrians

   d. Slippery When Wet

94. When are you allowed to pass a vehicle on the right on a two-lane road?

   a. Only in designated passing zones

   b. When the vehicle is making a left turn

   c. Only during rush hour traffic

   d. Never, unless directed by a police officer

95. What does a yellow and black diamond-shaped sign with the words "MERGE LEFT" indicate?

   a. Divided Highway Ends

   b. Merging Traffic

c. No Passing Zone

d. Lane Reduction Ahead

96. What does a red and white triangular sign with the words "RIGHT TURN AHEAD" indicate?

a. Right-of-Way Ahead

b. Warning - Right Turn Ahead

c. No Right Turn

d. Stop Sign Ahead

97. When are you allowed to make a U-turn at an intersection with a traffic signal?

a. Only if there is a "U-Turn Permitted" sign

b. When the way is clear of oncoming traffic and pedestrians

c. Only during nighttime

d. Never, unless directed by a traffic officer

98. What does a blue rectangular sign with white lettering and a white symbol of a gas pump indicate?

a. Gas Station Ahead

b. Rest Area Ahead

c. Fueling Station for Emergency Vehicles

d. No Gasoline Service

99. When must you use your vehicle's headlights?

a. Only during nighttime hours

b. Only during inclement weather or when visibility is reduced

c. Only in construction zones

d. Only when there are other vehicles around

100. What does a yellow and black circular sign with a picture of a traffic signal and the words "SIGNAL AHEAD" indicate?

a. Stop Sign Ahead

b. Yield Sign Ahead

c. Traffic Signal Ahead

d. Warning - Intersection Ahead

Answers:

91. c. Do Not Enter

92. b. To alert other drivers of your presence or to avoid a collision

93. c. Yield to Pedestrians

94. b. When the vehicle is making a left turn

95. b. Merging Traffic

96. b. Warning - Right Turn Ahead

97. b. When the way is clear of oncoming traffic and pedestrians

98. a. Gas Station Ahead

99. b. Only during inclement weather or when visibility is reduced

100. c. Traffic Signal Ahead

Explanation:

91. A white rectangular sign with black lettering and a red circle with a line through it indicates a prohibition, such as "Do Not Enter."

92. Use your vehicle's horn to alert other drivers of your presence or to avoid a collision.

93. A yellow and black circular sign with a picture of a person walking and the words "CROSSWALK" indicates the presence of a marked crosswalk, and drivers should yield to pedestrians.

94. Passing a vehicle on the right on a two-lane road is allowed when the vehicle in front is making a left turn.

95. A yellow and black diamond-shaped sign with the words "MERGE LEFT" indicates that drivers should merge left.

96. A red and white triangular sign with the words "RIGHT TURN AHEAD" warns drivers that a right turn is ahead.

97. U-turns at intersections with traffic signals are generally allowed when the way is clear of oncoming traffic and pedestrians.

98. A blue rectangular sign with white lettering and a white symbol of a gas pump indicates the presence of a gas station.

99. Use headlights during inclement weather or when visibility is reduced to enhance visibility for yourself and others on the road.

100. A yellow and black circular sign with a picture of a traffic signal and the words "SIGNAL AHEAD" indicates that a traffic signal is approaching.

Practice Test 3: Defensive Driving

1. What is defensive driving?

   a. Driving aggressively to assert dominance on the road

   b. Anticipating potential hazards and taking proactive measures to avoid accidents

   c. Ignoring other drivers to focus solely on your own actions

   d. Exceeding speed limits to stay ahead of traffic

2. When should you check your mirrors while driving defensively?

   a. Only when changing lanes

   b. Before and after turning

   c. Every 10 minutes

   d. Only when approaching an intersection

3. What is the primary goal of maintaining a safe following distance?

   a. To save fuel

   b. To make other drivers uncomfortable

   c. To reduce the risk of a rear-end collision

   d. To set a new speed record

4. How can you minimize distractions while driving defensively?

   a. Engaging in lively conversations with passengers

   b. Adjusting the radio and navigation system while driving

   c. Using hands-free devices for phone calls

   d. Texting and checking emails at red lights

5. In defensive driving, what does scanning the road mean?

   a. Staring straight ahead without moving your eyes

   b. Glancing quickly at the road and then focusing on the dashboard

   c. Keeping your eyes moving and checking mirrors regularly

   d. Closing your eyes to relax and reduce stress

6. When merging onto a highway, what should you do to drive defensively?

a. Speed up and force your way into traffic

b. Slow down and wait for a large gap in traffic

c. Signal and adjust your speed to merge smoothly

d. Stop at the end of the ramp to assess traffic

7. What is the purpose of the "two-second rule" in defensive driving?

a. To determine the ideal following distance

b. To calculate your average speed

c. To estimate the time until your next rest stop

d. To decide when to change lanes

8. How can you be more visible to other drivers when driving defensively?

a. Drive with your headlights off during the day

b. Use your high-beam headlights at all times

c. Keep your vehicle clean and ensure all lights are working

d. Stay in the blind spots of other drivers

9. What should you do if another driver is displaying aggressive behavior?

a. Match their aggression to assert dominance

b. Ignore their behavior and continue driving normally

c. Retaliate with offensive gestures or actions

d. Report aggressive driving to law enforcement

10. What does it mean to have a "360-degree awareness" while driving defensively?

a. Focusing solely on the road ahead

b. Being aware of everything happening around your vehicle

c. Ignoring the rearview mirror to reduce distractions

d. Keeping your eyes fixed on the dashboard

Answers:

1. b. Anticipating potential hazards and taking proactive measures to avoid accidents

2. b. Before and after turning

3. c. To reduce the risk of a rear-end collision

4. c. Using hands-free devices for phone calls

5. c. Keeping your eyes moving and checking mirrors regularly

6. c. Signal and adjust your speed to merge smoothly

7. a. To determine the ideal following distance

8. c. Keep your vehicle clean and ensure all lights are working

9. d. Report aggressive driving to law enforcement

10. b. Being aware of everything happening around your vehicle

Explanation:

1. Defensive driving involves anticipating potential hazards and taking proactive measures to avoid accidents.

2. Checking mirrors before and after turning helps maintain awareness of surrounding traffic.

3. Maintaining a safe following distance reduces the risk of a rear-end collision.

4. Minimize distractions by using hands-free devices for phone calls rather than engaging in activities that take your eyes off the road.

5. Scanning the road in defensive driving means keeping your eyes moving and checking mirrors regularly to be aware of your surroundings.

6. When merging onto a highway, signal and adjust your speed to merge smoothly with traffic.

7. The "two-second rule" helps determine the ideal following distance to ensure a safe stopping distance.

8. To be more visible to other drivers, keep your vehicle clean, and ensure all lights are working.

9. In the face of aggressive behavior from another driver, report it to law enforcement rather than engaging in retaliation.

10. "360-degree awareness" means being aware of everything happening around your vehicle to enhance safety.

11. How does adjusting your speed in response to traffic conditions contribute to defensive driving?

    a. It allows you to drive faster and reach your destination sooner

    b. It helps maintain a safe and appropriate speed for the current conditions

    c. It prevents other drivers from passing you

    d. It helps conserve fuel by driving at a constant speed

12. What should you do if you are being tailgated by another vehicle while driving defensively?

    a. Increase your speed to create more space

    b. Brake suddenly to warn the tailgater

    c. Move to the right lane to allow them to pass

d. Ignore the tailgater and continue at your current speed

13. In defensive driving, how should you approach a yellow traffic light?

   a. Speed up to clear the intersection before it turns red

   b. Stop abruptly to avoid running the red light

   c. Slow down and prepare to stop, unless it is unsafe to do so

   d. Ignore the traffic light and proceed through the intersection

14. Why is it important to be aware of the road conditions in defensive driving?

   a. To challenge your driving skills in adverse conditions

   b. To determine the best time to race on the road

   c. To adjust your driving to the current weather and road conditions

   d. To test the capabilities of your vehicle

15. What is the significance of a yellow and black diamond-shaped sign with the words "LANE ENDS MERGE LEFT" in defensive driving?

   a. It indicates a designated lane for aggressive driving

   b. It warns of a lane ending, requiring a merge to the left

   c. It designates a lane for high-speed driving

   d. It marks the beginning of a passing zone

16. When driving defensively, why is it crucial to watch for pedestrians and bicyclists at intersections?

   a. To challenge pedestrians and bicyclists to a race

   b. To ignore their presence and prioritize vehicular traffic

   c. To anticipate their movements and yield the right-of-way when necessary

   d. To accelerate through intersections to avoid congestion

17. How does practicing patience contribute to defensive driving?

   a. It allows you to drive aggressively and assert dominance on the road

   b. It helps you avoid aggressive behavior and stay calm in traffic

   c. It encourages tailgating to pressure other drivers

   d. It leads to excessive speeding to reach your destination quickly

18. What is the purpose of a "blind spot" in defensive driving?

a. To challenge drivers to navigate through blind spots

b. To test the peripheral vision of the driver

c. To hide other vehicles from view, making lane changes dangerous

d. To provide a safe area for aggressive driving maneuvers

19. Why is it important to maintain a consistent speed in heavy traffic when driving defensively?

a. To challenge other drivers to keep up with your pace

b. To create gaps for aggressive lane changes

c. To reduce the risk of rear-end collisions and promote smoother traffic flow

d. To exceed speed limits and reach the destination faster

20. What defensive driving technique should you use when approaching a large commercial vehicle, such as a truck or bus?

a. Drive closely behind to maintain visibility

b. Pass quickly on either side to avoid congestion

c. Stay in their blind spots to avoid being noticed

d. Give them plenty of space and avoid lingering beside them

Answers:

11. b. It helps maintain a safe and appropriate speed for the current conditions

12. c. Move to the right lane to allow them to pass

13. c. Slow down and prepare to stop, unless it is unsafe to do so

14. c. To adjust your driving to the current weather and road conditions

15. b. It warns of a lane ending, requiring a merge to the left

16. c. To anticipate their movements and yield the right-of-way when necessary

17. b. It helps you avoid aggressive behavior and stay calm in traffic

18. c. To hide other vehicles from view, making lane changes dangerous

19. c. To reduce the risk of rear-end collisions and promote smoother traffic flow

20. d. Give them plenty of space and avoid lingering beside them

Explanation:

11. Adjusting speed in response to traffic conditions helps maintain a safe and appropriate speed for the current situation.

12. When being tailgated, move to the right lane to allow the faster driver to pass safely.

13. Approach a yellow traffic light by slowing down and preparing to stop, unless it is unsafe to do so.

14. Being aware of road conditions is crucial to adjust your driving to the current weather and road conditions for safety.

15. A yellow and black diamond-shaped sign with the words "LANE ENDS MERGE LEFT" warns of a lane ending, requiring a merge to the left.

16. In defensive driving, watch for pedestrians and bicyclists at intersections to anticipate their movements and yield the right-of-way when necessary.

17. Practicing patience helps avoid aggressive behavior, contributing to a calm and safe driving experience.

18. A "blind spot" hides other vehicles from view, making lane changes dangerous if not checked properly.

19. Maintaining a consistent speed in heavy traffic reduces the risk of rear-end collisions and promotes smoother traffic flow.

20. When approaching large commercial vehicles, give them plenty of space and avoid lingering beside them to ensure safety.

21. What defensive driving technique should you use when encountering a distracted driver on the road?
    a. Engage in distracting activities to compete with the other driver
    b. Maintain a safe following distance and be prepared for unpredictable behavior
    c. Tailgate to alert the distracted driver to your presence
    d. Overtake quickly to avoid being affected by their distraction

22. In defensive driving, what is the significance of a yellow and black circular sign with the words "SLOW" on it?
    a. It indicates a recommended speed limit for aggressive driving
    b. It warns of a speed trap ahead
    c. It suggests a reduced speed due to upcoming hazards or road conditions
    d. It designates a zone for high-speed driving

23. How does keeping a steady speed contribute to defensive driving?
    a. It makes you stand out on the road
    b. It allows for unpredictable speed changes to surprise other drivers
    c. It promotes smooth traffic flow and reduces the risk of accidents
    d. It helps maintain a competitive edge with surrounding drivers

24. When driving defensively, what is the purpose of using turn signals?

    a. To confuse other drivers about your intended actions

    b. To communicate your intentions and promote predictability

    c. To signal that you are in a rush and need the right-of-way

    d. To show off your vehicle's features to other drivers

25. How can defensive driving be affected by fatigue?

    a. Fatigue has no impact on defensive driving

    b. Fatigue increases alertness and responsiveness

    c. Fatigue impairs judgment, reaction time, and decision-making

    d. Fatigue enhances concentration and focus

26. What is the proper defensive driving response to adverse weather conditions, such as heavy rain or snow?

    a. Drive at maximum speed to minimize the time spent in adverse conditions

    b. Use hazard lights to signal your presence to other drivers

    c. Reduce speed, increase following distance, and use headlights for visibility

    d. Ignore the weather conditions and maintain a constant speed

27. How can proper maintenance of your vehicle contribute to defensive driving?

    a. Neglecting maintenance increases the vehicle's performance

    b. Regular maintenance ensures the vehicle stands out on the road

    c. Proper maintenance enhances vehicle reliability and reduces breakdowns

    d. Maintaining a dirty vehicle promotes visibility

28. Why is it important to avoid aggressive gestures or verbal confrontations in defensive driving?

    a. Aggressive gestures assert dominance on the road

    b. They make driving more entertaining for other motorists

    c. Aggressive behavior can escalate conflicts and lead to road rage incidents

    d. They are essential for effective communication with other drivers

29. What does a white rectangular sign with black lettering and a red circle with a line through it indicate in defensive driving?

a. No U-turn

b. Speed Limit Ahead

c. Yield to Pedestrians

d. Stop Sign Ahead

30. How does staying alert to the actions of other drivers contribute to defensive driving?

a. It distracts you from focusing on your own driving

b. It allows you to mimic the actions of other drivers for variety

c. It helps anticipate potential hazards and react accordingly

d. It encourages you to challenge other drivers on the road

Answers:

21. b. Maintain a safe following distance and be prepared for unpredictable behavior

22. c. It suggests a reduced speed due to upcoming hazards or road conditions

23. c. It promotes smooth traffic flow and reduces the risk of accidents

24. b. To communicate your intentions and promote predictability

25. c. Fatigue impairs judgment, reaction time, and decision-making

26. c. Reduce speed, increase following distance, and use headlights for visibility

27. c. Proper maintenance enhances vehicle reliability and reduces breakdowns

28. c. Aggressive behavior can escalate conflicts and lead to road rage incidents

29. a. No U-turn

30. c. It helps anticipate potential hazards and react accordingly

Explanation:

21. When encountering a distracted driver, maintain a safe following distance and be prepared for unpredictable behavior.

22. A yellow and black circular sign with the words "SLOW" suggests a reduced speed due to upcoming hazards or road conditions.

23. Keeping a steady speed promotes smooth traffic flow and reduces the risk of accidents.

24. Using turn signals in defensive driving communicates your intentions to other drivers, promoting predictability.

25. Fatigue impairs judgment, reaction time, and decision-making, negatively impacting defensive driving.

26. In adverse weather conditions, such as heavy rain or snow, reduce speed, increase following distance, and use headlights for visibility.

27. Proper maintenance enhances vehicle reliability and reduces breakdowns, contributing to defensive driving.

28. Avoiding aggressive gestures or verbal confrontations is essential in defensive driving to prevent conflicts and road rage incidents.

29. A white rectangular sign with black lettering and a red circle with a line through it indicates "No U-turn."

30. Staying alert to the actions of other drivers helps anticipate potential hazards and react accordingly, contributing to defensive driving.

31. How can you minimize blind spots when driving defensively?

    a. Frequently adjust your mirrors and check them before making lane changes

    b. Keep your mirrors stationary to maintain a consistent view of the road

    c. Ignore blind spots and rely solely on peripheral vision

    d. Install wide-angle lenses on your side mirrors

32. In defensive driving, what does the term "tailgating" refer to?

    a. Following other drivers too closely

    b. Driving with the rear gate of your vehicle open

    c. Tailoring your driving style to match the vehicle in front

    d. Letting others pass you on the road

33. How does defensive driving contribute to fuel efficiency?

    a. Driving at maximum speed to reach the destination quickly

    b. Accelerating quickly at traffic signals

    c. Maintaining a steady speed and avoiding aggressive driving behaviors

    d. Ignoring maintenance to save on fuel costs

34. When driving defensively, what is the purpose of adjusting your speed in construction zones?

    a. To challenge construction workers with high-speed driving

    b. To reduce fuel efficiency

    c. To comply with speed limits and ensure the safety of workers and other drivers

d. To complete the construction zone as quickly as possible

35. How can proper hand placement on the steering wheel contribute to defensive driving?
    a. Gripping the steering wheel with one hand for flexibility
    b. Placing hands at 12 and 6 o'clock positions to maintain control
    c. Keeping hands close to the center for quick maneuvers
    d. Using only one hand on the steering wheel

36. What should you do when encountering a school bus with flashing red lights and an extended stop sign arm in defensive driving?
    a. Overtake the school bus quickly to avoid delays
    b. Ignore the flashing lights and proceed with caution
    c. Stop at a safe distance until the bus retracts the stop sign arm and turns off the flashing lights
    d. Honk the horn to alert the bus driver

37. How does defensive driving relate to sharing the road with vulnerable road users, such as pedestrians and cyclists?
    a. Ignore vulnerable road users to prioritize vehicular traffic
    b. Challenge vulnerable road users with assertive driving
    c. Anticipate the movements of vulnerable road users and yield the right-of-way
    d. Encourage vulnerable road users to use designated lanes

38. What is the significance of a yellow and black triangular sign with the words "SLOW DOWN" in defensive driving?
    a. It indicates a speed limit for aggressive driving
    b. It warns of a speed trap ahead
    c. It suggests reducing speed due to upcoming hazards or road conditions
    d. It designates a zone for high-speed driving

39. How can using proper signaling enhance defensive driving?
    a. Signaling is unnecessary in defensive driving
    b. It communicates your intentions, promoting predictability and safety
    c. Signaling is reserved for emergencies only
    d. Using signals distracts other drivers on the road

40. In defensive driving, what is the purpose of being aware of your surroundings?

    a. To focus solely on your own driving without considering other road users

    b. To challenge other drivers to navigate around you

    c. To anticipate potential hazards and react accordingly

    d. To ignore the actions of other drivers

Answers:

31. a. Frequently adjust your mirrors and check them before making lane changes

32. a. Following other drivers too closely

33. c. Maintaining a steady speed and avoiding aggressive driving behaviors

34. c. To comply with speed limits and ensure the safety of workers and other drivers

35. b. Placing hands at 12 and 6 o'clock positions to maintain control

36. c. Stop at a safe distance until the bus retracts the stop sign arm and turns off the flashing lights

37. c. Anticipate the movements of vulnerable road users and yield the right-of-way

38. c. It suggests reducing speed due to upcoming hazards or road conditions

39. b. It communicates your intentions, promoting predictability and safety

40. c. To anticipate potential hazards and react accordingly

Explanation:

31. Minimize blind spots by frequently adjusting your mirrors and checking them before making lane changes.

32. "Tailgating" in defensive driving refers to following other drivers too closely.

33. Defensive driving contributes to fuel efficiency by maintaining a steady speed and avoiding aggressive driving behaviors.

34. Adjust your speed in construction zones in defensive driving to comply with speed limits and ensure the safety of workers and other drivers.

35. Proper hand placement on the steering wheel, such as placing hands at 12 and 6 o'clock positions, contributes to maintaining control.

36. When encountering a school bus with flashing red lights and an extended stop sign arm, stop at a safe distance until the bus retracts the stop sign arm and turns off the flashing lights.

37. Defensive driving involves anticipating the movements of vulnerable road users, such as pedestrians and cyclists, and yielding the right-of-way.

38. A yellow and black triangular sign with the words "SLOW DOWN" suggests reducing speed due to upcoming hazards or road conditions in defensive driving.

39. Using proper signaling in defensive driving communicates your intentions, promoting predictability and safety.

40. Being aware of your surroundings in defensive driving helps anticipate potential hazards and react accordingly for safety.

Absolutely, let's proceed with more questions on defensive driving:

41. Why is it important to avoid using your mobile phone while driving in defensive driving?

  a. Using a mobile phone enhances focus and concentration

  b. Mobile phones do not impact driving performance

  c. Distracted driving increases the risk of accidents

  d. Using a mobile phone showcases multitasking skills

42. How does maintaining a cushion of space around your vehicle contribute to defensive driving?

  a. It creates a barrier to prevent other drivers from passing

  b. It allows for aggressive driving maneuvers in tight spaces

  c. It provides room for maneuvering and reaction time in emergencies

  d. Maintaining a cushion of space is unnecessary in defensive driving

43. What does the term "defensive parking" mean?

  a. Parking in restricted areas to save time

  b. Parking far away from other vehicles to avoid scratches

  c. Ignoring parking regulations to assert dominance

  d. Parking aggressively to secure the best spots

44. How can awareness of road signs contribute to defensive driving?

  a. Road signs are irrelevant to defensive driving

  b. Understanding road signs helps navigate safely and anticipate upcoming conditions

  c. Road signs are only for decorative purposes

  d. Ignoring road signs promotes assertive driving

45. When approaching an intersection in defensive driving, what should you do if the traffic signal is malfunctioning?

a. Speed through the intersection without stopping

b. Treat the intersection as a four-way stop and proceed with caution

c. Ignore the malfunction and follow the flow of traffic

d. Honk the horn to alert other drivers

46. How does defensive driving relate to dealing with aggressive or road rage behaviors from other drivers?

a. Respond with aggression to assert dominance

b. Ignoring aggressive behavior promotes road safety

c. Escalate conflicts by retaliating with offensive gestures

d. Report aggressive or road rage behaviors to law enforcement

47. What does it mean to "cover the brake" in defensive driving?

a. Slamming on the brake pedal aggressively

b. Keeping your foot on the brake pedal at all times

c. Applying light pressure to the brake pedal to reduce reaction time

d. Ignoring the brake pedal to maintain speed

48. In defensive driving, how can you manage the glare from headlights of oncoming vehicles at night?

a. Stare directly at the headlights to challenge the other driver

b. Wear sunglasses to reduce glare

c. Look slightly to the right and use the edge of the road as a guide

d. Flash your high beams in retaliation

49. What is the purpose of a white rectangular sign with black lettering and a black symbol of a pedestrian in defensive driving?

a. No Parking Zone

b. Pedestrian Crossing

c. No U-turn

d. Speed Limit Ahead

50. How does defensive driving relate to the proper use of turn signals?

a. Turn signals are optional in defensive driving

b. Using turn signals communicates your intentions, promoting predictability

c. Turn signals should only be used during emergency situations

d. Using turn signals is reserved for aggressive driving maneuvers

Answers:

41. c. Distracted driving increases the risk of accidents

42. c. It provides room for maneuvering and reaction time in emergencies

43. b. Parking far away from other vehicles to avoid scratches

44. b. Understanding road signs helps navigate safely and anticipate upcoming conditions

45. b. Treat the intersection as a four-way stop and proceed with caution

46. b. Ignoring aggressive behavior promotes road safety

47. c. Applying light pressure to the brake pedal to reduce reaction time

48. c. Look slightly to the right and use the edge of the road as a guide

49. b. Pedestrian Crossing

50. b. Using turn signals communicates your intentions, promoting predictability

Explanation:

41. Using a mobile phone while driving in defensive driving increases the risk of accidents due to distracted driving.

42. Maintaining a cushion of space around your vehicle in defensive driving provides room for maneuvering and reaction time in emergencies.

43. "Defensive parking" involves parking far away from other vehicles to avoid scratches and potential collisions.

44. Awareness of road signs in defensive driving helps navigate safely and anticipate upcoming conditions on the road.

45. When approaching an intersection with a malfunctioning traffic signal in defensive driving, treat it as a four-way stop and proceed with caution.

46. In dealing with aggressive or road rage behaviors from other drivers, ignoring such behavior promotes road safety.

47. "Covering the brake" in defensive driving means applying light pressure to the brake pedal to reduce reaction time.

48. To manage the glare from headlights of oncoming vehicles at night in defensive driving, look slightly to the right and use the edge of the road as a guide.

49. A white rectangular sign with black lettering and a black symbol of a pedestrian indicates a pedestrian crossing in defensive driving.

50. Proper use of turn signals in defensive driving communicates your intentions, promoting predictability and safety on the road.

Practice Test 4: Vehicle Operation and Maintenance

1. What should you do before starting your vehicle's engine?

   a. Check the fuel level

   b. Adjust the side mirrors

   c. Engage the parking brake

   d. Honk the horn

2. When is the best time to check the engine oil level in your vehicle?

   a. After a long drive

   b. When the engine is cold

   c. During heavy rain

   d. When the fuel tank is nearly empty

3. How often should you check your vehicle's tire pressure?

   a. Once a year

   b. Only when the tire looks flat

   c. Monthly or as recommended in the owner's manual

   d. Every time you fill up the gas tank

4. What is the purpose of the radiator in a vehicle?

   a. To store excess engine oil

   b. To cool the engine by dissipating heat

   c. To filter contaminants from the fuel

   d. To provide additional braking power

5. How can you improve fuel efficiency in your vehicle?

   a. Drive at maximum speed

   b. Accelerate quickly from a complete stop

   c. Keep your vehicle well-maintained

   d. Inflate tires to the maximum recommended pressure

6. What is the recommended interval for changing the engine oil in most vehicles?

a. Every 1,000 miles

b. Every 10,000 miles

c. Every 3,000 to 5,000 miles or as specified in the owner's manual

d. Only when the engine starts making noise

7. What should you do if your vehicle's brakes feel soft or spongy when you apply them?

a. Ignore it; soft brakes are normal

b. Pump the brake pedal to build up pressure

c. Decrease the brake fluid level

d. Have the brake system inspected immediately

8. How does the air filter contribute to the performance of your vehicle?

a. It increases fuel efficiency

b. It provides a pleasant fragrance inside the vehicle

c. It filters the air entering the engine, preventing contaminants

d. It regulates the vehicle's air conditioning

9. What is the purpose of the alternator in a vehicle?

a. To charge the battery and power electrical components when the engine is running

b. To cool the engine

c. To convert fuel into energy for the vehicle

d. To regulate the transmission fluid

10. How can you extend the life of your vehicle's brakes?

a. Brake aggressively to maintain responsiveness

b. Ignore unusual sounds when braking

c. Downshift to slow down instead of using the brakes

d. Apply the brakes suddenly in emergency situations

Answers:

1. c. Engage the parking brake

2. b. When the engine is cold

3. c. Monthly or as recommended in the owner's manual

4. b. To cool the engine by dissipating heat

5. c. Keep your vehicle well-maintained

6. c. Every 3,000 to 5,000 miles or as specified in the owner's manual

7. d. Have the brake system inspected immediately

8. c. It filters the air entering the engine, preventing contaminants

9. a. To charge the battery and power electrical components when the engine is running

10. c. Downshift to slow down instead of using the brakes

Explanation:

1. Before starting your vehicle's engine, engage the parking brake to prevent unintentional movement.

2. Check the engine oil level when the engine is cold for a more accurate measurement.

3. Check your vehicle's tire pressure monthly or as recommended in the owner's manual to ensure optimal performance.

4. The radiator's purpose is to cool the engine by dissipating heat generated during operation.

5. Keeping your vehicle well-maintained, including regular maintenance, contributes to improved fuel efficiency.

6. Most vehicles require an oil change every 3,000 to 5,000 miles or as specified in the owner's manual.

7. If your vehicle's brakes feel soft or spongy, have the brake system inspected immediately for potential issues.

8. The air filter filters the air entering the engine, preventing contaminants and contributing to optimal engine performance.

9. The alternator charges the battery and powers electrical components when the engine is running.

10. To extend the life of your vehicle's brakes, downshift to slow down instead of relying solely on the brakes, especially in emergency situations.

11. What does the term "tread depth" refer to when discussing tires on a vehicle?

   a. The width of the tire

   b. The thickness of the tire's sidewall

   c. The depth of the tire's grooves and patterns

   d. The overall diameter of the tire

12. Why is it important to rotate your vehicle's tires regularly?

   a. To show even wear patterns across all tires

   b. To increase fuel efficiency

   c. To decrease traction on the road

d. To extend the life of the spare tire

13. When should you replace windshield wiper blades on your vehicle?

   a. Only when they completely fall apart

   b. When you notice streaks or smearing during operation

   c. Every five years, regardless of condition

   d. Only in extreme weather conditions

14. How does proper wheel alignment contribute to vehicle safety and performance?

   a. It improves fuel efficiency

   b. It prevents uneven tire wear and ensures straight tracking

   c. It enhances the vehicle's top speed

   d. It reduces the overall weight of the vehicle

15. What is the purpose of the timing belt in a vehicle's engine?

   a. To regulate the vehicle's timing for optimal performance

   b. To measure the time it takes to accelerate from 0 to 60 mph

   c. To assist in steering the vehicle

   d. To control the temperature of the engine

16. How often should you check the level of your vehicle's transmission fluid?

   a. Once a year

   b. Only when experiencing transmission problems

   c. Regularly, as specified in the owner's manual

   d. Only when the vehicle is brand new

17. What does the term "blinker fluid" refer to in the context of a vehicle?

   a. A fictional substance used in jokes and pranks

   b. A critical fluid for the proper functioning of the vehicle's turn signals

   c. An essential component of the air conditioning system

   d. A lubricant for the vehicle's suspension system

18. Why is it important to maintain the proper level of engine coolant in your vehicle?

   a. To enhance the vehicle's sound system

b. To prevent the engine from overheating and ensure efficient operation

c. To improve fuel efficiency

d. To increase the vehicle's top speed

19. How does the proper inflation of tires contribute to vehicle safety and performance?

a. It decreases fuel efficiency

b. It promotes even tire wear and optimal traction on the road

c. It increases the risk of a blowout

d. It has no impact on vehicle safety

20. What should you do if your vehicle's check engine light comes on?

a. Ignore it; check engine lights are often false alarms

b. Immediately visit a qualified mechanic for a diagnostic check

c. Disconnect the battery to reset the light

d. Only address it if the vehicle starts experiencing performance issues

Answers:

11. c. The depth of the tire's grooves and patterns

12. a. To show even wear patterns across all tires

13. b. When you notice streaks or smearing during operation

14. b. It prevents uneven tire wear and ensures straight tracking

15. a. To regulate the vehicle's timing for optimal performance

16. c. Regularly, as specified in the owner's manual

17. a. A fictional substance used in jokes and pranks

18. b. To prevent the engine from overheating and ensure efficient operation

19. b. It promotes even tire wear and optimal traction on the road

20. b. Immediately visit a qualified mechanic for a diagnostic check

Explanation:

11. Tread depth refers to the depth of the tire's grooves and patterns, crucial for maintaining traction on the road.

12. Regularly rotating tires ensures even wear patterns across all tires, extending their life and improving performance.

13. Worn windshield wiper blades can affect visibility; replace them when you notice streaks or smearing.

14. Proper wheel alignment prevents uneven tire wear and ensures the vehicle tracks straight, contributing to safety and performance.

15. The timing belt regulates the timing of the engine's components for optimal performance.

16. Check the level of transmission fluid regularly, as specified in the owner's manual, to ensure proper functioning.

17. "Blinker fluid" is a fictional substance used in jokes and pranks, not an actual vehicle component.

18. Maintaining the proper level of engine coolant prevents the engine from overheating and ensures efficient operation.

19. Properly inflated tires promote even wear and optimal traction on the road, contributing to safety and performance.

20. If the check engine light comes on, it's essential to visit a qualified mechanic for a diagnostic check to identify potential issues.

21. What is the purpose of the serpentine belt in a vehicle?

    a. To control the vehicle's steering

    b. To power the air conditioning system

    c. To regulate the vehicle's suspension

    d. To drive various engine components such as the alternator and water pump

22. How often should you replace the cabin air filter in your vehicle?

    a. Once every two years

    b. Only when you notice a strange odor inside the vehicle

    c. Regularly, as recommended in the owner's manual

    d. Only when the air conditioning is not cooling properly

23. What should you do if you notice a sudden loss of tire pressure while driving?

    a. Continue driving normally; the pressure will correct itself

    b. Immediately pull over to the side of the road

    c. Increase your speed to reach a service station quickly

    d. Pump the brakes aggressively to stabilize the vehicle

24. How can you maximize the lifespan of your vehicle's battery?

    a. Regularly discharge the battery completely before recharging

    b. Avoid using electronic accessories when the engine is off

c. Keep the battery exposed to direct sunlight for extended periods

d. Use the highest-powered electrical accessories at all times

25. What does the term "cruise control" refer to in vehicle operation?

a. A feature that automatically steers the vehicle

b. A system that maintains a constant speed set by the driver

c. A control for adjusting the vehicle's suspension

d. A mechanism for enhancing fuel efficiency

26. Why is it important to check the alignment of your vehicle's headlights regularly?

a. To blind other drivers on the road

b. To ensure proper visibility at night and avoid dazzling other drivers

c. To conserve energy and extend the life of the headlights

d. Headlight alignment has no impact on vehicle safety

27. What is the purpose of the fuel filter in a vehicle?

a. To enhance the vehicle's exhaust system

b. To purify the air entering the engine

c. To filter contaminants from the fuel before reaching the engine

d. To control the vehicle's transmission

28. How can you properly dispose of used motor oil from your vehicle?

a. Pour it down the drain

b. Dispose of it in regular household trash

c. Take it to a recycling center or an authorized collection facility

d. Store it in your garage for future use

29. Why should you avoid overloading your vehicle beyond its specified capacity?

a. Overloading improves fuel efficiency

b. It has no impact on the vehicle's performance

c. Overloading can lead to poor handling, increased braking distances, and tire failure

d. It helps in achieving better acceleration

30. What does the term "hydroplaning" mean in the context of driving?

a. A technique for efficient fuel consumption

b. The vehicle losing traction on wet surfaces and skimming over the water

c. A method of conserving water resources during the wash

d. A feature that improves the vehicle's hydrodynamic performance

Answers:

21. d. To drive various engine components such as the alternator and water pump

22. c. Regularly, as recommended in the owner's manual

23. b. Immediately pull over to the side of the road

24. b. Avoid using electronic accessories when the engine is off

25. b. A system that maintains a constant speed set by the driver

26. b. To ensure proper visibility at night and avoid dazzling other drivers

27. c. To filter contaminants from the fuel before reaching the engine

28. c. Take it to a recycling center or an authorized collection facility

29. c. Overloading can lead to poor handling, increased braking distances, and tire failure

30. b. The vehicle losing traction on wet surfaces and skimming over the water

Explanation:

21. The serpentine belt drives various engine components such as the alternator and water pump.

22. Replace the cabin air filter regularly, as recommended in the owner's manual, for optimal air quality inside the vehicle.

23. If you notice a sudden loss of tire pressure while driving, immediately pull over to the side of the road to address the issue.

24. Maximize the lifespan of your vehicle's battery by avoiding the use of electronic accessories when the engine is off.

25. Cruise control is a system that maintains a constant speed set by the driver for convenience during highway driving.

26. Checking the alignment of your vehicle's headlights regularly ensures proper visibility at night and prevents dazzling other drivers.

27. The fuel filter in a vehicle filters contaminants from the fuel before reaching the engine, promoting efficient operation.

28. Properly dispose of used motor oil by taking it to a recycling center or an authorized collection facility to protect the environment.

29. Overloading your vehicle beyond its specified capacity can lead to poor handling, increased braking distances, and tire failure.

30. Hydroplaning occurs when a vehicle loses traction on wet surfaces and skims over the water, leading to reduced control.

31. What is the recommended frequency for checking and replacing the spark plugs in your vehicle?

    a. Every 2,000 miles

    b. Every 50,000 to 100,000 miles or as specified in the owner's manual

    c. Only if the vehicle experiences difficulty starting

    d. Once a month

32. How does the proper adjustment of side mirrors contribute to safe driving?

    a. It reduces fuel consumption

    b. It eliminates blind spots and improves visibility around the vehicle

    c. It enhances the vehicle's top speed

    d. It has no impact on driving safety

33. Why is it important to maintain a clean and unobstructed windshield?

    a. To enhance the vehicle's aesthetics

    b. To reduce fuel efficiency

    c. To improve visibility and ensure safe driving

    d. To prevent overheating of the engine

34. What is the purpose of the catalytic converter in a vehicle's exhaust system?

    a. To cool the exhaust gases before release

    b. To increase engine noise for a sportier sound

    c. To reduce harmful emissions by converting them into less harmful substances

    d. To regulate the vehicle's fuel injection system

35. How can you identify if your vehicle's suspension system needs attention?

    a. By the color of the suspension components

    b. By the smell of the vehicle's interior

    c. Unusual noises, vibrations, or uneven tire wear

    d. Only during extreme weather conditions

36. What is the purpose of the power steering fluid in a vehicle?

   a. To regulate the engine's power output

   b. To enhance the vehicle's braking system

   c. To lubricate the transmission components

   d. To assist in steering by reducing the effort required

37. How often should you replace the brake fluid in your vehicle?

   a. Once every 10,000 miles

   b. Only when the brakes start making noise

   c. Regularly, as specified in the owner's manual

   d. Brake fluid does not require replacement

38. Why is it essential to secure loose items within your vehicle before driving?

   a. To improve fuel efficiency

   b. To enhance the vehicle's aerodynamics

   c. To prevent distractions and potential hazards during driving

   d. To achieve a smoother ride

39. How does proper tire rotation contribute to extending the life of your vehicle's tires?

   a. It prevents tire rotation and ensures even wear

   b. It promotes uneven tire wear for better traction

   c. It maintains consistent wear patterns across all tires

   d. Tire rotation has no impact on tire lifespan

40. What is the purpose of the owner's manual in your vehicle?

   a. To serve as a decorative item in the glove compartment

   b. To provide detailed information on the vehicle's operation, maintenance, and safety features

   c. To be used as a notepad for personal reminders

   d. To store personal belongings

Answers:

31. b. Every 50,000 to 100,000 miles or as specified in the owner's manual

32. b. It eliminates blind spots and improves visibility around the vehicle

33. c. To improve visibility and ensure safe driving

34. c. To reduce harmful emissions by converting them into less harmful substances

35. c. Unusual noises, vibrations, or uneven tire wear

36. d. To assist in steering by reducing the effort required

37. c. Regularly, as specified in the owner's manual

38. c. To prevent distractions and potential hazards during driving

39. c. It maintains consistent wear patterns across all tires

40. b. To provide detailed information on the vehicle's operation, maintenance, and safety features

Explanation:

31. Check and replace spark plugs every 50,000 to 100,000 miles or as specified in the owner's manual for optimal engine performance.

32. Properly adjusted side mirrors eliminate blind spots and improve overall visibility around the vehicle.

33. A clean and unobstructed windshield is crucial to improve visibility and ensure safe driving.

34. The catalytic converter reduces harmful emissions by converting them into less harmful substances in the vehicle's exhaust system.

35. Identify suspension issues by paying attention to unusual noises, vibrations, or uneven tire wear.

36. Power steering fluid assists in steering by reducing the effort required, contributing to smoother and more controlled steering.

37. Replace brake fluid regularly, as specified in the owner's manual, to maintain proper brake function and safety.

38. Securing loose items within your vehicle is essential to prevent distractions and potential hazards during driving.

39. Proper tire rotation maintains consistent wear patterns across all tires, extending their life and improving performance.

40. The owner's manual provides detailed information on the vehicle's operation, maintenance, and safety features, serving as a valuable reference guide for the owner.

41. What does the term "engine knocking" refer to in a vehicle?

    a. A rhythmic noise indicating a well-functioning engine

    b. The sound of the engine starting

    c. An abnormal banging or pinging noise from the engine

    d. The engine's response to high-speed acceleration

42. How often should you check the condition of your vehicle's drive belts?

    a. Only when you hear a squeaking noise

    b. Monthly or as specified in the owner's manual

    c. Once a year during the vehicle's annual inspection

    d. Drive belts do not require regular checks

43. What is the purpose of the differential in a vehicle's drivetrain?

    a. To increase fuel efficiency

    b. To provide power to the rear wheels while allowing them to rotate at different speeds

    c. To regulate the vehicle's suspension

    d. To control the transmission fluid temperature

44. Why should you avoid "riding the brake" while driving downhill?

    a. It conserves fuel

    b. It extends the life of the brake pads

    c. It reduces the risk of engine overheating

    d. It can cause the brakes to overheat and lose effectiveness

45. How does the tire pressure monitoring system (TPMS) contribute to vehicle safety?

    a. It enhances fuel efficiency

    b. It prevents tire punctures

    c. It alerts the driver when tire pressure is too low

    d. It improves the vehicle's top speed

46. What is the purpose of the alternator belt in a vehicle?

    a. To regulate the engine's power output

    b. To provide power to the alternator for charging the battery

    c. To control the vehicle's air conditioning system

    d. To increase the vehicle's acceleration

47. How can you prevent corrosion on your vehicle's battery terminals?

    a. Apply a layer of grease to the terminals

    b. Pour water over the terminals regularly

    c. Ignore the terminals; corrosion is unavoidable

d. Disconnect the battery when the vehicle is not in use

48. Why is it important to replace a damaged or missing gas cap on your vehicle?

    a. It improves engine performance

    b. It prevents fuel from evaporating and reduces harmful emissions

    c. It enhances the vehicle's aerodynamics

    d. Gas caps have no impact on vehicle operation

49. What is the purpose of the oxygen sensor in a vehicle's exhaust system?

    a. To regulate the vehicle's suspension

    b. To control the transmission fluid temperature

    c. To improve fuel efficiency

    d. To monitor and reduce harmful emissions

50. How can you prevent your vehicle's engine from overheating in hot weather?

    a. Drive at maximum speed to increase air circulation

    b. Keep the windows closed to retain cool air inside the vehicle

    c. Use the air conditioning sparingly to avoid straining the engine

    d. Ensure proper coolant levels and cooling system function

Answers:

41. c. An abnormal banging or pinging noise from the engine

42. b. Monthly or as specified in the owner's manual

43. b. To provide power to the rear wheels while allowing them to rotate at different speeds

44. d. It can cause the brakes to overheat and lose effectiveness

45. c. It alerts the driver when tire pressure is too low

46. b. To provide power to the alternator for charging the battery

47. a. Apply a layer of grease to the terminals

48. b. It prevents fuel from evaporating and reduces harmful emissions

49. d. To monitor and reduce harmful emissions

50. d. Ensure proper coolant levels and cooling system function

Explanation:

41. Engine knocking refers to an abnormal banging or pinging noise from the engine, which can indicate issues with fuel or ignition timing.

42. Check the condition of drive belts monthly or as specified in the owner's manual to ensure proper operation and prevent breakdowns.

43. The differential provides power to the rear wheels while allowing them to rotate at different speeds, improving maneuverability.

44. "Riding the brake" downhill can cause the brakes to overheat and lose effectiveness; use engine braking or downshifting instead.

45. The Tire Pressure Monitoring System (TPMS) alerts the driver when tire pressure is too low, enhancing safety and preventing issues.

46. The alternator belt provides power to the alternator for charging the battery and supporting electrical components.

47. Prevent corrosion on battery terminals by applying a layer of grease, protecting against the corrosive effects of battery acid.

48. Replacing a damaged or missing gas cap prevents fuel from evaporating, reducing harmful emissions and maintaining proper fuel system pressure.

49. The oxygen sensor monitors and reduces harmful emissions in the exhaust system, contributing to environmental protection.

50. Prevent engine overheating in hot weather by ensuring proper coolant levels and maintaining the cooling system's function.

Practice Test 5: Parking and Maneuvering

1. What is the proper way to parallel park your vehicle?
   a. Park at an angle to the curb with the front wheels turned away
   b. Park parallel to the curb, leaving at least 18 inches between your vehicle and the curb
   c. Park with the rear wheels against the curb
   d. Park on the sidewalk to allow more space for other vehicles

2. When parking uphill with a curb, how should you position your front wheels?
   a. Turn the wheels away from the curb
   b. Turn the wheels toward the curb
   c. Keep the wheels straight
   d. It doesn't matter how the wheels are positioned

3. What does the term "head-in parking" mean?
   a. Parking with the front of your vehicle facing the exit
   b. Parking with the rear of your vehicle facing the exit
   c. Parking perpendicular to the curb
   d. Parking with the windows down

4. When parking downhill with a curb, how should you position your front wheels?
   a. Turn the wheels away from the curb
   b. Turn the wheels toward the curb
   c. Keep the wheels straight
   d. Turn the vehicle around and park facing uphill

5. What is the purpose of the two-second rule when following another vehicle?
   a. To estimate the distance between your vehicle and the one in front
   b. To calculate the time it takes for your vehicle to come to a complete stop
   c. To determine the speed of the vehicle in front of you
   d. To ensure you are not following too closely

6. What does a blue parking curb indicate?

a. Loading zone

b. Handicap parking

c. Short-term parking

d. Tourist parking

7. How should you approach a roundabout?

    a. Speed up to merge quickly

    b. Always yield to traffic in the roundabout

    c. Honk your horn to alert other drivers

    d. Drive in the opposite direction to exit

8. What does a white painted curb signify?

    a. Loading zone

    b. No parking or stopping at any time

    c. Short-term parking

    d. Reserved for emergency vehicles only

9. How should you handle a flashing red traffic signal at an intersection?

    a. Treat it as a stop sign; come to a complete stop and proceed when safe

    b. Proceed without stopping; flashing red signals have no significance

    c. Slow down and proceed cautiously

    d. Yield the right-of-way to cross traffic

10. What is the purpose of the crosshatched lines near handicapped parking spaces?

    a. Designate the area for loading and unloading

    b. Indicate the space is reserved for pregnant women

    c. Provide additional space for wheelchair ramps and mobility devices

    d. Serve as a decorative element

Answers:

1. b. Park parallel to the curb, leaving at least 18 inches between your vehicle and the curb

2. a. Turn the wheels away from the curb

3. a. Parking with the front of your vehicle facing the exit

4. b. Turn the wheels toward the curb

5. d. To ensure you are not following too closely

6. b. Handicap parking

7. b. Always yield to traffic in the roundabout

8. b. No parking or stopping at any time

9. a. Treat it as a stop sign; come to a complete stop and proceed when safe

10. c. Provide additional space for wheelchair ramps and mobility devices

Explanation:

1. When parallel parking, park parallel to the curb, leaving at least 18 inches between your vehicle and the curb.

2. When parking uphill with a curb, turn the wheels away from the curb to prevent the vehicle from rolling into the street.

3. Head-in parking refers to parking with the front of your vehicle facing the exit.

4. When parking downhill with a curb, turn the wheels toward the curb to prevent the vehicle from rolling into the street.

5. The two-second rule helps ensure you are not following the vehicle in front of you too closely, providing a safe following distance.

6. A blue parking curb typically indicates handicap parking spaces.

7. When approaching a roundabout, always yield to traffic in the roundabout and proceed with caution.

8. A white painted curb signifies no parking or stopping at any time.

9. When facing a flashing red traffic signal at an intersection, treat it as a stop sign and proceed when safe.

10. Crosshatched lines near handicapped parking spaces provide additional space for wheelchair ramps and mobility devices.

11. What does the term "three-point turn" mean?

   a. A technique for turning left at a three-way intersection

   b. A method of turning around in a limited space by making three separate maneuvers

   c. A maneuver to avoid an obstacle in the road

   d. A type of parallel parking technique

12. How should you park when facing uphill without a curb?

   a. Turn the wheels away from the road

   b. Turn the wheels toward the road

   c. Keep the wheels straight

d. Park with the rear of your vehicle facing uphill

13. What does a yellow painted curb indicate?
    a. No parking or stopping at any time
    b. Loading zone
    c. Short-term parking
    d. Reserved for school buses only

14. When executing a U-turn, what should you be aware of?
    a. U-turns are prohibited in most areas
    b. Always use the center lane if available
    c. Check for signs prohibiting U-turns and yield to oncoming traffic
    d. U-turns are only allowed at night

15. How should you park when facing downhill without a curb?
    a. Turn the wheels away from the road
    b. Turn the wheels toward the road
    c. Keep the wheels straight
    d. Park with the front of your vehicle facing downhill

16. What does the term "angle parking" refer to?
    a. Parking at a 90-degree angle to the curb
    b. Parking parallel to the curb
    c. Parking on a hill with the wheels turned
    d. Parking within designated lines at an angle

17. When making a left turn at an intersection with a green light, what should you do?
    a. Proceed without stopping
    b. Yield to oncoming traffic and pedestrians
    c. Honk your horn to clear the intersection
    d. Speed up to clear the intersection quickly

18. How should you approach a parking space when parallel parking?
    a. Approach the space from the rear

b. Approach the space from the front

c. Approach the space at a 45-degree angle

d. Approach the space at a 90-degree angle

19. What is the purpose of a loading zone?

   a. Reserved for vehicles with large loads or cargo

   b. A designated area for unloading passengers or goods

   c. A zone where speed limits are higher for loading vehicles

   d. Reserved for vehicles with a loading dock

20. When should you use your turn signals when parking on the side of the road?

   a. Only when other vehicles are present

   b. Use them after parking to indicate you are leaving

   c. Use them before pulling over and while parked

   d. Turn signals are not necessary when parking

Answers:

11. b. A method of turning around in a limited space by making three separate maneuvers

12. a. Turn the wheels away from the road

13. b. Loading zone

14. c. Check for signs prohibiting U-turns and yield to oncoming traffic

15. b. Turn the wheels toward the road

16. a. Parking at a 90-degree angle to the curb

17. b. Yield to oncoming traffic and pedestrians

18. b. Approach the space from the front

19. b. A designated area for unloading passengers or goods

20. c. Use them before pulling over and while parked

Explanation:

11. A three-point turn involves turning around in a limited space by making three separate maneuvers, often used on narrow streets.

12. When facing uphill without a curb, turn the wheels away from the road to prevent the vehicle from rolling into the street.

13. A yellow painted curb typically indicates a loading zone.

14. When executing a U-turn, check for signs prohibiting U-turns and yield to oncoming traffic before making the maneuver.

15. When facing downhill without a curb, turn the wheels toward the road to prevent the vehicle from rolling into the street.

16. Angle parking refers to parking at a 90-degree angle to the curb within designated lines.

17. When making a left turn at an intersection with a green light, yield to oncoming traffic and pedestrians.

18. When parallel parking, approach the space from the front to align your vehicle properly with the curb.

19. A loading zone is a designated area for unloading passengers or goods, often near businesses or delivery areas.

20. Use your turn signals before pulling over and while parked to indicate your intention to other road users.

21. What does the term "kerb parking" refer to?

   a. Parking on the sidewalk

   b. Parking with the wheels touching the curb

   c. Parking at a distance from the curb

   d. Parking with the engine running

22. When approaching a stop sign, how far back from the stop line should you stop your vehicle?

   a. At least 5 feet

   b. Right at the stop line

   c. Far enough to see cross traffic

   d. Approximately 10 feet

23. What is the purpose of a roundabout?

   a. To allow vehicles to travel at higher speeds

   b. To reduce traffic congestion and improve safety

   c. To create a decorative element in the road

   d. To discourage left turns

24. How should you park in a space designated for disabled individuals (handicapped parking)?

   a. Park briefly for a quick errand if you don't see any disabled individuals nearby

   b. Park only if you have a disabled permit or license plate

c. Park if the space is available, regardless of your disability status

d. Park only during off-peak hours

25. What does a broken yellow line on the road indicate?

   a. No passing allowed

   b. Passing allowed with caution

   c. Passing allowed only on the left

   d. Passing allowed only on the right

26. How should you park when facing uphill with no curb or shoulder on the road?

   a. Turn the wheels away from the road

   b. Turn the wheels toward the road

   c. Keep the wheels straight

   d. Park with the rear of your vehicle facing uphill

27. What is the purpose of the white painted stop line at an intersection?

   a. A decorative element

   b. To indicate the crosswalk

   c. To assist pedestrians in crossing

   d. To mark the stopping point for vehicles

28. What does the term "NO PARKING ZONE" mean?

   a. Parking is allowed during specific hours

   b. Parking is not allowed at any time

   c. Parking is allowed for commercial vehicles only

   d. Parking is allowed, but only for a short duration

29. When executing a three-point turn, what is the correct sequence of maneuvers?

   a. Pull over to the right, reverse, turn, and continue in the opposite direction

   b. Pull over to the left, reverse, turn, and continue in the opposite direction

   c. Turn around in a circle to change direction

   d. Pull over, turn on your hazard lights, and wait for traffic to clear

30. How should you approach a parking space when angle parking?

a. Approach the space at a 90-degree angle

b. Approach the space from the front at a slight angle

c. Approach the space from the rear at a slight angle

d. Approach the space at a 45-degree angle

Answers:

21. b. Parking with the wheels touching the curb

22. c. Far enough to see cross traffic

23. b. To reduce traffic congestion and improve safety

24. b. Park only if you have a disabled permit or license plate

25. b. Passing allowed with caution

26. a. Turn the wheels away from the road

27. d. To mark the stopping point for vehicles

28. b. Parking is not allowed at any time

29. b. Pull over to the left, reverse, turn, and continue in the opposite direction

30. d. Approach the space at a 45-degree angle

Explanation:

21. Kerb parking refers to parking with the wheels touching the curb for proper alignment.

22. When approaching a stop sign, stop far enough back to see cross traffic and provide a clear view.

23. Roundabouts are designed to reduce traffic congestion, improve safety, and facilitate continuous traffic flow.

24. Parking in a space designated for disabled individuals is only allowed if you have a disabled permit or license plate.

25. A broken yellow line on the road indicates passing is allowed with caution.

26. When facing uphill with no curb or shoulder, turn the wheels away from the road to prevent the vehicle from rolling into traffic.

27. The white painted stop line at an intersection marks the stopping point for vehicles, enhancing traffic flow and safety.

28. A "NO PARKING ZONE" means parking is not allowed at any time in the designated area.

29. During a three-point turn, pull over to the left, reverse, turn, and continue in the opposite direction.

30. When angle parking, approach the space at a 45-degree angle for optimal positioning within designated lines.

31. What should you do when approaching a school bus with its red lights flashing and the stop arm extended?

    a. Continue driving without stopping

    b. Slow down and proceed with caution

    c. Stop at least 20 feet away and wait until the bus moves or the red lights stop flashing

    d. Overtake the bus quickly to avoid delays

32. How far away from a fire hydrant should you park?

    a. At least 5 feet

    b. At least 10 feet

    c. At least 15 feet

    d. Park directly in front of the fire hydrant

33. When parking downhill with a curb, how should you position your front wheels?

    a. Turn the wheels away from the curb

    b. Turn the wheels toward the curb

    c. Keep the wheels straight

    d. Turn the vehicle around and park facing uphill

34. What does the term "crosswalk" mean?

    a. A designated area for crossing the street, marked with white lines

    b. A place for vehicles to cross each other's paths

    c. A decorative pattern on the road

    d. A walkway reserved for pedestrians

35. How should you park when facing uphill with no curb or shoulder on the road?

    a. Turn the wheels away from the road

    b. Turn the wheels toward the road

    c. Keep the wheels straight

    d. Park with the rear of your vehicle facing uphill

36. What does the term "head-out parking" mean?

    a. Parking with the front of your vehicle facing the road

    b. Parking with the rear of your vehicle facing the road

c. Parking perpendicular to the curb

d. Parking with the windows down

37. How should you approach a parking space when parallel parking?

    a. Approach the space from the rear

    b. Approach the space from the front

    c. Approach the space at a 45-degree angle

    d. Approach the space at a 90-degree angle

38. What does a solid yellow line on the road indicate?

    a. No passing allowed

    b. Passing allowed with caution

    c. Passing allowed only on the left

    d. Passing allowed only on the right

39. When should you use your hazard lights while parked?

    a. Whenever you're parked for an extended period

    b. When parked on a hill

    c. Only during inclement weather or low visibility conditions

    d. Hazard lights should not be used while parked

40. How should you park when facing downhill with a curb?

    a. Turn the wheels away from the curb

    b. Turn the wheels toward the curb

    c. Keep the wheels straight

    d. Turn the vehicle around and park facing uphill

Answers:

31. c. Stop at least 20 feet away and wait until the bus moves or the red lights stop flashing

32. c. At least 15 feet

33. b. Turn the wheels toward the curb

34. a. A designated area for crossing the street, marked with white lines

35. b. Turn the wheels toward the road

36. a. Parking with the front of your vehicle facing the road

37. b. Approach the space from the front

38. a. No passing allowed

39. c. Only during inclement weather or low visibility conditions

40. a. Turn the wheels away from the curb

Explanation:

31. When approaching a school bus with its red lights flashing and the stop arm extended, stop at least 20 feet away and wait until the bus moves or the red lights stop flashing.

32. Park at least 15 feet away from a fire hydrant to ensure access for emergency vehicles.

33. When parking downhill with a curb, turn the wheels toward the curb to prevent the vehicle from rolling into the street.

34. A crosswalk is a designated area for pedestrians to cross the street, typically marked with white lines.

35. When facing uphill with no curb or shoulder, turn the wheels toward the road to prevent the vehicle from rolling into traffic.

36. Head-out parking involves parking with the front of your vehicle facing the road.

37. When parallel parking, approach the space from the front to align your vehicle properly with the curb.

38. A solid yellow line on the road indicates no passing allowed.

39. Use hazard lights only during inclement weather or low visibility conditions while parked to alert other drivers to your presence.

40. When facing downhill with a curb, turn the wheels away from the curb to prevent the vehicle from rolling into the street.

41. What is the purpose of a loading zone?

    a. Reserved for vehicles with large loads or cargo

    b. A designated area for unloading passengers or goods

    c. A zone where speed limits are higher for loading vehicles

    d. Reserved for vehicles with a loading dock

42. How should you park when facing uphill with a curb?

    a. Turn the wheels away from the curb

    b. Turn the wheels toward the curb

    c. Keep the wheels straight

    d. Turn the vehicle around and park facing downhill

43. What does a white painted curb signify?

    a. Loading zone

    b. No parking or stopping at any time

    c. Short-term parking

    d. Reserved for emergency vehicles only

44. How should you park in a space designated for disabled individuals (handicapped parking)?

    a. Park briefly for a quick errand if you don't see any disabled individuals nearby

    b. Park only if you have a disabled permit or license plate

    c. Park if the space is available, regardless of your disability status

    d. Park only during off-peak hours

45. What does the term "crosswalk" mean?

    a. A designated area for crossing the street, marked with white lines

    b. A place for vehicles to cross each other's paths

    c. A decorative pattern on the road

    d. A walkway reserved for pedestrians

46. How should you park when facing downhill with a curb?

    a. Turn the wheels away from the curb

    b. Turn the wheels toward the curb

    c. Keep the wheels straight

    d. Turn the vehicle around and park facing uphill

47. What does a broken yellow line on the road indicate?

    a. No passing allowed

    b. Passing allowed with caution

    c. Passing allowed only on the left

    d. Passing allowed only on the right

48. How should you approach a parking space when parallel parking?

    a. Approach the space from the rear

    b. Approach the space from the front

    c. Approach the space at a 45-degree angle

d. Approach the space at a 90-degree angle

49. What does a solid yellow line on the road indicate?

   a. No passing allowed

   b. Passing allowed with caution

   c. Passing allowed only on the left

   d. Passing allowed only on the right

50. How should you park in a space designated for motorcycle parking?

   a. Park parallel to the curb

   b. Park at an angle to the curb

   c. Park perpendicular to the curb

   d. Park in any direction as long as the space is occupied

Answers:

41. b. A designated area for unloading passengers or goods

42. a. Turn the wheels away from the curb

43. b. No parking or stopping at any time

44. b. Park only if you have a disabled permit or license plate

45. a. A designated area for crossing the street, marked with white lines

46. b. Turn the wheels toward the curb

47. b. Passing allowed with caution

48. b. Approach the space from the front

49. a. No passing allowed

50. a. Park parallel to the curb

Explanation:

41. Loading zones are designated areas for unloading passengers or goods, often found near businesses or delivery areas.

42. When facing uphill with a curb, turn the wheels away from the curb to prevent the vehicle from rolling into the street.

43. A white painted curb signifies no parking or stopping at any time.

44. Parking in a space designated for disabled individuals is only allowed if you have a disabled permit or license plate.

45. A crosswalk is a designated area marked with white lines for pedestrians to cross the street safely.

46. When facing downhill with a curb, turn the wheels toward the curb to prevent the vehicle from rolling into the street.

47. A broken yellow line on the road indicates passing is allowed with caution.

48. When parallel parking, approach the space from the front to align your vehicle properly with the curb.

49. A solid yellow line on the road indicates no passing allowed.

50. In a space designated for motorcycle parking, park parallel to the curb for efficient use of space and orderly parking.

Practice Test 6: Special License Considerations

1. What is the minimum age requirement for obtaining a learner's permit in California?

   a. 16 years old

   b. 17 years old

   c. 18 years old

   d. 15 and a half years old

2. How long must a new resident in California with an out-of-state driver's license apply for a California driver's license?

   a. Within 10 days

   b. Within 20 days

   c. Within 30 days

   d. Within 40 days

3. What does a Class C driver's license in California allow you to operate?

   a. Regular passenger cars and trucks

   b. Motorcycles

   c. Commercial vehicles

   d. Recreational vehicles only

4. In California, what is the minimum age requirement for obtaining a Class C driver's license?

   a. 16 years old

   b. 18 years old

   c. 21 years old

   d. 25 years old

5. What is the primary purpose of a Commercial Driver's License (CDL)?

   a. To operate a motorcycle

   b. To operate a regular passenger car

   c. To operate commercial vehicles such as trucks and buses

   d. To operate recreational vehicles

6. When applying for a motorcycle license in California, what age requirement must be met?

    a. 16 years old

    b. 18 years old

    c. 21 years old

    d. 25 years old

7. How often must commercial drivers in California undergo a medical examination to maintain their CDL?

    a. Every year

    b. Every two years

    c. Every three years

    d. Only when renewing the CDL

8. What is the minimum age requirement for obtaining a Commercial Driver's License (CDL) in California?

    a. 18 years old

    b. 21 years old

    c. 25 years old

    d. 30 years old

9. What is the Blood Alcohol Concentration (BAC) limit for commercial drivers operating a commercial vehicle in California?

    a. 0.02%

    b. 0.04%

    c. 0.06%

    d. 0.08%

10. What is the purpose of a motorcycle helmet in California?

    a. To enhance the rider's fashion

    b. To protect against head injuries in case of an accident

    c. To provide shade from the sun

    d. To comply with local fashion trends

Answers:

1. d. 15 and a half years old

2. c. Within 30 days

3. a. Regular passenger cars and trucks

4. a. 16 years old

5. c. To operate commercial vehicles such as trucks and buses

6. a. 16 years old

7. b. Every two years

8. b. 21 years old

9. b. 0.04%

10. b. To protect against head injuries in case of an accident

Explanation:

1. The minimum age requirement for obtaining a learner's permit in California is 15 and a half years old.

2. New residents in California with an out-of-state driver's license must apply for a California driver's license within 30 days.

3. A Class C driver's license in California allows you to operate regular passenger cars and trucks.

4. The minimum age requirement for obtaining a Class C driver's license is 16 years old.

5. The primary purpose of a Commercial Driver's License (CDL) is to operate commercial vehicles such as trucks and buses.

6. When applying for a motorcycle license in California, the minimum age requirement is 16 years old.

7. Commercial drivers in California must undergo a medical examination every two years to maintain their CDL.

8. The minimum age requirement for obtaining a Commercial Driver's License (CDL) in California is 21 years old.

9. The Blood Alcohol Concentration (BAC) limit for commercial drivers operating a commercial vehicle in California is 0.04%.

10. The purpose of a motorcycle helmet in California is to protect against head injuries in case of an accident.

11. What type of endorsement may be required for commercial drivers transporting hazardous materials?

    a. H Endorsement

    b. X Endorsement

    c. T Endorsement

    d. Z Endorsement

12. If you are under 18 years old, what is the requirement for obtaining a provisional driver's license in California?

   a. Complete at least 50 hours of supervised driving practice

   b. Pass the written test only

   c. Have a clean driving record with no violations

   d. Complete a driver's education course only

13. What does an M1 endorsement on a California driver's license signify?

   a. Allows the operation of regular passenger cars and trucks

   b. Permits the operation of commercial vehicles

   c. Allows the operation of motorcycles

   d. Indicates a medical restriction

14. How often must drivers age 70 and older renew their driver's license in California?

   a. Every two years

   b. Every four years

   c. Every six years

   d. Every eight years

15. What is the minimum age requirement for obtaining a motorcycle learner's permit in California?

   a. 16 years old

   b. 17 years old

   c. 18 years old

   d. 21 years old

16. What is the purpose of an H Endorsement on a Commercial Driver's License (CDL)?

   a. Allows the operation of hazardous materials vehicles

   b. Permits the operation of passenger vehicles

   c. Allows the operation of motorcycles

   d. Indicates a medical restriction

17. When applying for a provisional driver's license in California, what restrictions apply during the first 12 months?

a. No restrictions

b. No passengers under 20 years old unless accompanied by a licensed driver age 25 or older

c. No nighttime driving

d. No driving on weekends

18. What is the minimum age requirement for obtaining a Commercial Driver's License (CDL) with a hazardous materials endorsement in California?

a. 18 years old

b. 21 years old

c. 25 years old

d. 30 years old

19. What is the purpose of an X Endorsement on a Commercial Driver's License (CDL)?

a. Allows the operation of hazardous materials vehicles

b. Permits the operation of passenger vehicles

c. Allows the operation of motorcycles

d. Indicates a medical restriction

20. What type of license is required for operating a motorized scooter in California?

a. Class C driver's license

b. Class M1 or M2 motorcycle license

c. Class A driver's license

d. No license is required

Answers:

11. b. X Endorsement

12. a. Complete at least 50 hours of supervised driving practice

13. c. Allows the operation of motorcycles

14. b. Every four years

15. a. 16 years old

16. a. Allows the operation of hazardous materials vehicles

17. b. No passengers under 20 years old unless accompanied by a licensed driver age 25 or older

18. b. 21 years old

19. a. Allows the operation of hazardous materials vehicles

20. d. No license is required

Explanation:

11. An X Endorsement on a Commercial Driver's License (CDL) is required for drivers transporting hazardous materials.

12. If you are under 18 years old, you must complete at least 50 hours of supervised driving practice to obtain a provisional driver's license in California.

13. An M1 endorsement on a California driver's license allows the operation of motorcycles.

14. Drivers age 70 and older must renew their driver's license in California every four years.

15. The minimum age requirement for obtaining a motorcycle learner's permit in California is 16 years old.

16. An H Endorsement on a CDL allows the operation of hazardous materials vehicles.

17. When applying for a provisional driver's license in California, there are restrictions during the first 12 months, including no passengers under 20 years old unless accompanied by a licensed driver age 25 or older.

18. The minimum age requirement for obtaining a CDL with a hazardous materials endorsement in California is 21 years old.

19. An X Endorsement on a CDL allows the operation of hazardous materials vehicles.

20. No license is required for operating a motorized scooter in California.

21. What is the minimum age requirement for obtaining a commercial driver's license (CDL) with a school bus endorsement in California?

    a. 18 years old
    b. 21 years old
    c. 25 years old
    d. 30 years old

22. What type of license is required for operating an electric scooter in California?

    a. Class C driver's license
    b. Class M1 or M2 motorcycle license
    c. Class A driver's license
    d. No license is required

23. What does an M2 endorsement on a California driver's license signify?

a. Allows the operation of regular passenger cars and trucks

b. Permits the operation of commercial vehicles

c. Allows the operation of motorcycles

d. Indicates a medical restriction

24. What is the purpose of a T Endorsement on a commercial driver's license (CDL)?

a. Allows the operation of hazardous materials vehicles

b. Permits the operation of passenger vehicles

c. Allows the operation of tank vehicles

d. Indicates a medical restriction

25. What is the minimum age requirement for obtaining a Class B commercial driver's license (CDL) in California?

a. 18 years old

b. 21 years old

c. 25 years old

d. 30 years old

26. If a driver under 18 years old is convicted of using a wireless device while driving, what penalty may be imposed?

a. Fine and community service

b. License suspension

c. Points on the driving record

d. All of the above

27. What is the minimum age requirement for obtaining a Class A commercial driver's license (CDL) in California?

a. 18 years old

b. 21 years old

c. 25 years old

d. 30 years old

28. When applying for a provisional driver's license in California, what passenger restrictions apply during the first 12 months?

a. No restrictions

b. No passengers under 20 years old unless accompanied by a licensed driver age 25 or older

c. No nighttime driving

d. No driving on weekends

29. What does a tank endorsement on a commercial driver's license (CDL) allow the driver to operate?

a. Hazardous materials vehicles

b. Passenger vehicles

c. Tank vehicles

d. Motorcycles

30. In California, what is the minimum age requirement for obtaining a Class M1 or M2 motorcycle license?

a. 16 years old

b. 18 years old

c. 21 years old

d. 25 years old

Answers:

21. a. 18 years old

22. d. No license is required

23. c. Allows the operation of motorcycles

24. c. Allows the operation of tank vehicles

25. b. 21 years old

26. d. All of the above

27. b. 21 years old

28. b. No passengers under 20 years old unless accompanied by a licensed driver age 25 or older

29. c. Tank vehicles

30. a. 16 years old

Explanation:

21. The minimum age requirement for obtaining a CDL with a school bus endorsement in California is 18 years old.

22. No license is required for operating an electric scooter in California.

23. An M2 endorsement on a California driver's license allows the operation of motorcycles.

24. A T Endorsement on a CDL allows the operation of tank vehicles.

25. The minimum age requirement for obtaining a Class B CDL in California is 21 years old.

26. If a driver under 18 is convicted of using a wireless device while driving, they may face fines, community service, license suspension, or points on their driving record.

27. The minimum age requirement for obtaining a Class A CDL in California is 21 years old.

28. When applying for a provisional driver's license in California, there are restrictions on passengers during the first 12 months, including no passengers under 20 years old unless accompanied by a licensed driver age 25 or older.

29. A tank endorsement on a CDL allows the driver to operate tank vehicles.

30. The minimum age requirement for obtaining a Class M1 or M2 motorcycle license in California is 16 years old.

31. What is the minimum age requirement for obtaining a Class B commercial driver's license (CDL) with a passenger endorsement in California?

   a. 18 years old

   b. 21 years old

   c. 25 years old

   d. 30 years old

32. What type of license is required for operating a motorized skateboard in California?

   a. Class C driver's license

   b. Class M1 or M2 motorcycle license

   c. Class A driver's license

   d. No license is required

33. What does a passenger endorsement on a commercial driver's license (CDL) allow the driver to operate?

   a. Hazardous materials vehicles

   b. Passenger vehicles

   c. Tank vehicles

   d. Motorcycles

34. In California, what is the minimum age requirement for obtaining a Class C commercial driver's license (CDL)?

   a. 18 years old

   b. 21 years old

   c. 25 years old

   d. 30 years old

35. If a driver under 18 is convicted of driving under the influence (DUI), what penalty may be imposed?

   a. Fine and community service

   b. License suspension

   c. Points on the driving record

   d. All of the above

36. What is the minimum age requirement for obtaining a Class A commercial driver's license (CDL) with a passenger endorsement in California?

   a. 18 years old

   b. 21 years old

   c. 25 years old

   d. 30 years old

37. When applying for a motorcycle learner's permit in California, what is required in addition to passing the written test?

   a. Vision test

   b. Road test

   c. Medical examination

   d. All of the above

38. What type of license is required for operating an electric bicycle in California?

   a. Class C driver's license

   b. Class M1 or M2 motorcycle license

   c. Class A driver's license

   d. No license is required

39. What does an HME (Hazardous Materials Endorsement) on a commercial driver's license (CDL) indicate?

    a. Allows the operation of hazardous materials vehicles

    b. Permits the operation of passenger vehicles

    c. Allows the operation of motorcycles

    d. Indicates a medical restriction

40. In California, what is the minimum age requirement for obtaining a Class C commercial driver's license (CDL) with a hazardous materials endorsement?

    a. 18 years old

    b. 21 years old

    c. 25 years old

    d. 30 years old

Answers:

31. b. 21 years old

32. d. No license is required

33. b. Passenger vehicles

34. a. 18 years old

35. d. All of the above

36. b. 21 years old

37. d. All of the above

38. d. No license is required

39. a. Allows the operation of hazardous materials vehicles

40. b. 21 years old

Explanation:

31. The minimum age requirement for obtaining a Class B CDL with a passenger endorsement in California is 21 years old.

32. No license is required for operating a motorized skateboard in California.

33. A passenger endorsement on a CDL allows the driver to operate passenger vehicles.

34. The minimum age requirement for obtaining a Class C CDL in California is 18 years old.

35. If a driver under 18 is convicted of DUI, they may face fines, community service, license suspension, or points on their driving record.

36. The minimum age requirement for obtaining a Class A CDL with a passenger endorsement in California is 21 years old.

37. When applying for a motorcycle learner's permit in California, a vision test, road test, and medical examination are required in addition to passing the written test.

38. No license is required for operating an electric bicycle in California.

39. An HME (Hazardous Materials Endorsement) on a CDL indicates that the driver is allowed to operate hazardous materials vehicles.

40. The minimum age requirement for obtaining a Class C CDL with a hazardous materials endorsement in California is 21 years old.

Absolutely, let's continue with more questions on Special License Considerations:

41. What type of license is required for operating an e-scooter with a maximum speed of 20 mph in California?

    a. Class C driver's license

    b. Class M1 or M2 motorcycle license

    c. Class A driver's license

    d. No license is required

42. What is the minimum age requirement for obtaining a Class A commercial driver's license (CDL) with a tanker endorsement in California?

    a. 18 years old

    b. 21 years old

    c. 25 years old

    d. 30 years old

43. If a driver under 18 years old accumulates too many points on their driving record, what may happen?

    a. Required to attend traffic school

    b. License suspension

    c. Restricted driving hours

    d. All of the above

44. What is the minimum age requirement for obtaining a Class B commercial driver's license (CDL) with a hazmat endorsement in California?

    a. 18 years old

b. 21 years old

c. 25 years old

d. 30 years old

45. What does an M3 endorsement on a California driver's license signify?

a. Allows the operation of regular passenger cars and trucks

b. Permits the operation of commercial vehicles

c. Allows the operation of three-wheeled motorcycles

d. Indicates a medical restriction

46. What is the purpose of a P Endorsement on a commercial driver's license (CDL)?

a. Allows the operation of hazardous materials vehicles

b. Permits the operation of passenger vehicles

c. Allows the operation of motorcycles

d. Indicates a medical restriction

47. When applying for a motorcycle license in California, what is required in addition to passing the written test?

a. Vision test

b. Road test

c. Medical examination

d. All of the above

48. What type of license is required for operating an e-bike with a maximum speed of 28 mph in California?

a. Class C driver's license

b. Class M1 or M2 motorcycle license

c. Class A driver's license

d. No license is required

49. What does a Class M3 endorsement on a California driver's license allow the operator to ride?

a. Motorcycles only

b. Three-wheeled motorcycles only

c. Motorized scooters only

d. All of the above

50. What is the minimum age requirement for obtaining a Class C commercial driver's license (CDL) with a passenger endorsement in California?

    a. 18 years old

    b. 21 years old

    c. 25 years old

    d. 30 years old

Answers:

41. d. No license is required

42. b. 21 years old

43. b. License suspension

44. b. 21 years old

45. c. Allows the operation of three-wheeled motorcycles

46. c. Allows the operation of motorcycles

47. d. All of the above

48. d. No license is required

49. b. Three-wheeled motorcycles only

50. a. 18 years old

Explanation:

41. No license is required for operating an e-scooter with a maximum speed of 20 mph in California.

42. The minimum age requirement for obtaining a Class A CDL with a tanker endorsement in California is 21 years old.

43. If a driver under 18 accumulates too many points on their driving record, their license may be suspended.

44. The minimum age requirement for obtaining a Class B CDL with a hazmat endorsement in California is 21 years old.

45. An M3 endorsement on a California driver's license allows the operation of three-wheeled motorcycles.

46. A P Endorsement on a CDL allows the operation of passenger vehicles.

47. When applying for a motorcycle license in California, a vision test, road test, and medical examination are required in addition to passing the written test.

48. No license is required for operating an e-bike with a maximum speed of 28 mph in California.

49. A Class M3 endorsement on a California driver's license allows the operator to ride three-wheeled motorcycles only.

50. The minimum age requirement for obtaining a Class C CDL with a passenger endorsement in California is 18 years old.

CONCLUSION

As we near the conclusion of this thorough book, we hope it has been a beneficial resource in your quest to learn the laws of the road in California. The California DMV Written Test is an important step in acquiring your driver's license, and this book has been methodically prepared to provide you with the information and confidence you need to pass with flying colors.

Remember that driving is more than just a talent; it is a duty. This book provides knowledge that goes beyond the exam and serves as a basis for a lifetime of safe and responsible driving. Whether you are a novice driver or want to refresh your grasp of traffic regulations, we hope that the information offered will help you navigate California's various roads.

Always put safety first, be educated, and never stop learning. We wish you luck on your next test and many safe and pleasurable trips on the open road.

Drive safely!

Made in the USA
Middletown, DE
30 August 2024

60014394R00139